CLASSICS IN EDUCATION
Lawrence A. Cremin, General Editor

☆ ☆ ☆

THE REPUBLIC AND THE SCHOOL
Horace Mann on the Education of Free Men
Edited by Lawrence A. Cremin

AMERICAN IDEAS ABOUT ADULT EDUCATION
1710–1951
Edited by C. Hartley Grattan

DEWEY ON EDUCATION
Introduction and Notes by Martin S. Dworkin

THE SUPREME COURT AND EDUCATION
Edited by David Fellman

INTERNATIONAL EDUCATION
A Documentary History
Edited by David G. Scanlon

CRUSADE AGAINST IGNORANCE
Thomas Jefferson on Education
Edited by Gordon C. Lee

CHINESE EDUCATION UNDER COMMUNISM
Edited by Chang-tu Hu

CHARLES W. ELIOT AND POPULAR EDUCATION
Edited by Edward A. Krug

WILLIAM T. HARRIS ON EDUCATION
(in preparation)
Edited by Martin S. Dworkin

THE *EMILE* OF JEAN JACQUES ROUSSEAU
Selections
Translated and Edited by William Boyd

THE MINOR EDUCATIONAL WRITINGS OF
JEAN JACQUES ROUSSEAU
Selected and Translated by William Boyd

PSYCHOLOGY AND THE SCIENCE OF EDUCATION
Selected Writings of Edward L. Thorndike
Edited by Geraldine M. Joncich

THE NEW-ENGLAND PRIMER
Introduction by Paul Leicester Ford

BENJAMIN FRANKLIN ON EDUCATION
Edited by John Hardin Best

THE COLLEGES AND THE PUBLIC
1787–1862
Edited by Theodore Rawson Crane

TRADITIONS OF AFRICAN EDUCATION
Edited by David G. Scanlon

NOAH WEBSTER'S AMERICAN SPELLING BOOK
Introductory Essay by Henry Steele Commager

VITTORINO DA FELTRE
AND OTHER HUMANIST EDUCATORS
By William Harrison Woodward
Foreword by Eugene F. Rice, Jr.

DESIDERIUS ERASMUS
CONCERNING THE AIM AND METHOD
OF EDUCATION
By William Harrison Woodward
Foreword by Craig R. Thompson

JOHN LOCKE ON EDUCATION
Edited by Peter Gay

CATHOLIC EDUCATION IN AMERICA
A Documentary History
Edited by Neil G. McCluskey, S.J.

THE AGE OF THE ACADEMIES
Edited by Theodore R. Sizer

HEALTH, GROWTH, AND HEREDITY
G. Stanley Hall on Natural Education
Edited by Charles E. Strickland and Charles Burgess

TEACHER EDUCATION IN AMERICA
A Documentary History
Edited by Merle L. Borrowman

THE EDUCATED WOMAN IN AMERICA
Selected Writings of Catharine Beecher,
Margaret Fuller, and M. Carey Thomas
Edited by Barbara M. Cross

EMERSON ON EDUCATION
Selections
Edited by Howard Mumford Jones

ECONOMIC INFLUENCES UPON EDUCATIONAL
PROGRESS IN THE UNITED STATES, 1820–1850
By Frank Tracy Carlton
Foreword by Lawrence A. Cremin

QUINTILIAN ON EDUCATION
Selected and Translated by William M. Smail

ROMAN EDUCATION FROM CICERO
TO QUINTILIAN
By Aubrey Gwynn, S.J.

HERBERT SPENCER ON EDUCATION
Edited by Andreas M. Kazamias

JOHN LOCKE'S *OF THE CONDUCT
OF THE UNDERSTANDING*
Edited by Francis W. Garforth

STUDIES IN EDUCATION DURING THE
AGE OF THE RENAISSANCE, 1400–1600
By William Harrison Woodward
Foreword by Lawrence Stone

JOHN AMOS COMENIUS ON EDUCATION
Introduction by Jean Piaget

HUMANISM AND SOCIAL ORDER IN
TUDOR ENGLAND
By Fritz Caspari

VIVES' *INTRODUCTION TO WISDOM*
A Renaissance Textbook
Edited by Marian Leona Tobriner, S.N.J.M.

THE THEORY OF EDUCATION IN THE
REPUBLIC OF PLATO
By Richard Lewis Nettleship
Foreword by Robert McClintock

UTOPIANISM AND EDUCATION
Robert Owen and the Owenites
Edited by John F. C. Harrison

Vives'
Introduction to Wisdom

A RENAISSANCE TEXTBOOK

Edited, with an Introduction, by
MARIAN LEONA TOBRINER, S.N.J.M.

CLASSICS IN

No. 35

EDUCATION

TEACHERS COLLEGE PRESS
TEACHERS COLLEGE, COLUMBIA UNIVERSITY
NEW YORK

DEDICATION

Foreword

The traditional tendency to pass lightly over the contributions of Juan Luis Vives in discussions of English Renaissance education is at the least curious. Despite the efforts of William Harrison Woodward and Foster Watson to call the work of the brilliant Spanish humanist to the attention of twentieth-century scholars, few historians have paid proper heed to his teaching or his writing. Only in such recent studies as Eugene F. Rice's *The Renaissance Idea of Wisdom* (1958), Kenneth Charlton's *Education in Renaissance England* (1965), and Joan Simon's *Education and Society in Tudor England* (1966) have thoughtful appraisals of Vives been attempted. And, indeed, that a fundamental revaluation may be in the making is indicated by the fact that both Professor Rice and Mrs. Simon assign Vives an educational significance virtually equal to that of Erasmus.

Such an estimate would, of course, be thoroughly familiar to Vives' contemporaries, for they regarded the two men as two great symbols of the humanist cause. Like Erasmus, Vives typified the cosmopolitanism of the Renaissance, traveling as he did from Valencia to Paris to Louvain to London, and corresponding with scholars all over Western Europe. Like Erasmus, too, he manifested the catholicity of the Renaissance, writing freely on a vast variety of subjects, theological, scientific, and philosophical. And, like Erasmus, he demonstrated the centrality of education in the Renaissance: ultimately, all his thinking and writing converged on the problem of forming civilized men and women.

Most important, perhaps, Vives, like Erasmus, defined wisdom as piety, as Christian teaching translated into action. Erasmus had envisioned such wisdom as the outcome of education in his immensely popular *Enchiridion Militis Christiani (Manual of a Christian Knight)*, first published in 1503; Vives offered his *Introductio ad Sapientiam (Introduction to Wisdom)* as a means for achieving the goal. Wisdom in both treatises consists of virtue in combination with learning, embracing both moral precepts and the actions that derive from them. There is no more characteristic doctrine of the English Renaissance, and it is little wonder that Vives' textbook enjoyed a vogue that lasted well into the seventeenth century.

LAWRENCE A. CREMIN

Contents

Vives' *Introduction to Wisdom*

A RENAISSANCE TEXTBOOK

A Renaissance Textbook

By MARIAN LEONA TOBRINER, S.N.J.M.

THE FASHIONING OF A CHRISTIAN HUMANIST

During his lifetime (1492–1540) Northern Europe saluted Juan Luis Vives as another Quintilian, one destined to outshine and surpass even Erasmus.[1] Within fifty years of the Spanish humanist's premature death, publishers had put his Latin treatises through numerous translations in French, German, Italian, Polish, and Spanish.[2] A booming trade in English translations began in London. Nevertheless, while today's English and American general historians of the sixteenth century acknowledge him as a significant Renaissance thinker, an aura of dismissal hangs heavy over their pages.

Why this historical shade? Some believe it is because of his close relationship with Catherine of Aragon who carried to anonymity many with whom she was associated. Others refer to Vives' comparatively early death; others, to his relatively smaller literary production, if compared with the Renaissance giants; still others, to his Jewish

---

[1] The humanist of Rotterdam himself had once predicted this. See P. S. Allen, H. M. Allen, and H. W. Garrod, *Erasmi Epistolae* (11 vols.; Oxford, 1913–1947), III, Epistle 907, preface. [Hereafter "Epistle" is abbreviated to "Ep."]

[2] An incomplete bibliographical survey can be found in Adolfo y San Martín Bonilla, *Luis Vives y la Filosofía del Renacimiento* (Madrid, 1903), pp. 735–814.

origin and the obscurity reserved for non-Aryans by Western European bigotry.[3]

Nineteenth-century German scholarship, touching briefly on his writings and prestige, fired the enthusiasm of professional researchers.[4] To the advantage of the English-speaking world, during the first quarter of this century a professor of the history of education at the University College of Wales, Aberystwyth, became enamored with Vives. Foster Watson, with his studies in Valencia, Paris, and Bruges, provided a spirited but solitary revitalization of the Spanish humanist's works.[5] Presently, few scholars consider his theses in depth, extending them to English readers through commentary rather than through translation.[6] Current textbooks in the history of education refer to Vives in generous enough terms: a

---

[3] The latter position is held by Americo Castro, as stated in his *The Structure of Spanish History,* translated by Edmund L. King (Princeton, 1954), and maintained in an unpublished lecture at Loyola University, Los Angeles, on November 15, 1966.

[4] For several citations of German research see footnotes 1 and 2 of Marcia L. Colish, "The Mime of God: Vives on the Nature of Man," *Journal of the History of Ideas,* XXIII (1962), 3; also the extensive bibliography of Edward J. Baxter, S.J., "The Educational Thought of Juan Luis Vives" (unpublished doctoral dissertation, Harvard University, 1943).

[5] The author's unpublished doctoral dissertation, on which the present essay is based, cites twelve large works of Watson on Vives, admittedly an incomplete bibliography of all the Welshman's Renaissance studies. See "Juan Luis Vives' Introduction to Wisdom: A Renaissance Textbook—Its Author, Its Era, and Its Use" (Stanford University, 1966), pp. 474-475.

[6] See, for example, Colish, "The Mime of God," pp. 3–20; Baxter, "The Educational Thought of Juan Luis Vives"; Ruth Kuschmierz, "The Instruction of the Christian Woman: A Critical Edition of the Tudor Translations" (unpublished doctoral dissertation, University of Pittsburgh, 1961); Anne Margaret Riley, "Political Theories of J. L. Vives" (unpublished doctoral dissertation, University of New Mexico, 1955); and William Sinz, "The Elaboration of Vives' Treatises on the Arts," in *Renaissance Studies,* X (1963), 68–90.

leader of educational theory, "The Father of Modern Psychology," a major source of innovation in pedagogy from his own time through Herbert Spencer's.[7] Yet his works themselves are available in but small proportion to the English reader; errors prevail in the facts ascribed to his life; translations are generally limited to selected portions of the original volumes.

Quite the opposite condition prevailed in the sixteenth century. The seed of nationalism might germinate and flower; kingdoms evolving into modern states might exert partisan pressures on the intellectual life of citizens. Still, the tradition of an unfragmented Europe, the wistful memory of a once international state, imbued the thought and writings of the humanists. Ingenuously, the intellectual commonwealth stood unafraid of humanism across a border. What was there to hoard or defend when the arts and sciences converged on universal man? Vives might be from Valencia and Erasmus from Rotterdam, Budé from Paris and More from London. Nevertheless, literate society took for granted that such geographical divergencies enriched rather than hampered true scholarship.

Hence, it is no anomaly to discover that the exiled Spanish Vives would not only be tolerated in the Tudor world; he would, indeed, be inserted into the very center of its mental formation, its philosophy and pedagogy, its maxims and prayers. On the Continent his fellow-scholars turned to him in 1536 at the death of Erasmus and placed the leadership of letters in his hands.

[7] Foster Watson, "Father of Modern Psychology," in *Psychological Review,* XXII (1915), 333–353; Richard E. Gross, *Heritage of American Education* (New York, 1962), p. 21; and S. E. Frost, *Historical and Philosophical Foundations of Western Education* (Columbus, Ohio, 1966), pp. 182–184.

> Glorious son of glorious Valencia,
> Orator famous throughout the world,
> Immortal light of Latin literature,
> Glory of the Spanish nation,
> Honor of humanity . . .
> Not having completed his forty-fourth year
> Perforce will be the model and leader of all.[8]

The judgment of his peers suggests a reconstitution in twentieth-century estimates of the Spaniard's worth and influence.

Concerning the *Introductio ad Sapientiam (Introduction to Wisdom)*, specifically, Watson had remarked in 1922,

Of Vives' book there has been no modern re-issue except in Spain, in which country so recently as 1863, the *Introductio ad Sapientiam* was one of the books recommended by a royal ordinance for reading in the schools. There is a good reason why in England Vives' book should be accessible, seeing that there was an English translation made by Sir Richard Morison dedicated to the son of Thomas Cromwell. *A reprint would have double value, that of Vives' subject-matter, and as another example of the English employed in a version as early as 1540.* [Italics added.][9]

Here, in the present volume, and more than forty years later, the proposal is accepted. In Watson's spirit, this translation of the *Introductio ad Sapientiam,* first published in Louvain in 1524, is proffered in terms of Vives' content and of the Tudor mode of expression, the latter somewhat modernized for easier reading by a continued retranslation from the Latin.

---

[8] Henri de Vocht, *History of the Foundation and Rise of the Collegium Trilingue Lovaniense, 1517–1550* (4 vols.; Louvain, 1951–1955), III, 422–423, an excerpt from a eulogy for Erasmus. [Courtesy of Bureau du Recueil, University of Louvain.]

[9] Foster Watson, *Luis Vives: El Gran Valencian* (London, 1922), pp. 70–71. [Courtesy of The Hispanic Society of America.]

Supplementing the text is a consideration of Vives' life, in his personal, social, and religious milieu. The *Introductio* itself is briefly analyzed in its sixteenth-century tensions between an emerging science and the prevailing humanism. Some notes on its use as a textbook in English grammar schools reflect the phenomenon of expanding educational demands.[10] For the non-specialist, then, this essay proposes a brief survey of the Renaissance moment in history, and the specific contributions of Juan Luis Vives.

Man was not only the measure of all things, to Vives. He was much more: a richly endowed being whose excellence in society promised an eternal destiny in heaven. Less infected by a spirit of amoralism and relativism than those of his contemporaries,[11] his theories of psychology and philosophy, of religion and pedagogy, rooted man in the categorical relationship of creature to Creator. True, man was a marvel of thought and will; but he was, after all, just that—a man. Vives' recognition of this multi-faceted, yet integrated, condition makes of him an innovator, a humanist, a Christian—in fact, precisely a Christian humanist.

[10] Suggested titles from a wealth of works include John E. Neale, *The Elizabethan House of Commons* (London, 1949); Lawrence Stone, *The Crisis of the Aristocracy, 1558–1641* (New York, 1965); J. H. Hexter, *Reappraisals in History* (New York, 1961); Fritz Caspari, *Humanism and the Social Order in Tudor England* (Chicago, 1954; New York, 1968); Joan Simon, *Education and Society in Tudor England* (Cambridge, England, 1966); Kenneth Charlton, *Education in Renaissance England* (Toronto, 1965); and other studies buttressed by reference to political science, sociology, and economics, all elevating the examination of education in Tudor England to new levels of creative evaluation.

[11] Joseph Lortz, *The Reformation: A Problem for Today* (Westminster, Md., 1965), pp. 66–74. While the author admits Erasmus' excellence as a philologist and scholar, for example, he perceives a negative, destructive element in the humanist's religious orientations.

THE NEW EUROPE

Theorists and activists alike contributed to the complexity of sixteenth-century Europe. To illustrate, revolutionary opinions and measures in economic life broke through traditional restraints, feeding into powerful intellectual and religious streams.[12] Medici in the south and Fuggers in the north constructed banking systems which affected urban and rural markets alike. Manufacturing expanded into a domestic system which was to remain through most of the eighteenth century. Production and commerce, adapting to market conditions, assumed international airs. The rate and kind of consumption gave clue to social rank. A middle class appeared in cities at the same time, claiming lands used immemorially for agriculture and herding or newly diverted to systematized manufacturing.

Technologies expanded with proportionate swiftness and diversity.[13] Weaving, shipping, printing, papermaking, glassmaking, lumbering, mining, all advanced with a speed frightening by comparison with the ponderous stability of preceding centuries. At least one constant, yet extraneous, factor influenced the mechanics of this expansion. Physical catastrophes—such as the recurring visits of the Plague, excesses of heat and cold, floods from rivers and oceans—inevitably brought panic and frustration. The psychological effects from such elemental factors were reflected clearly in increasingly frequent peasant uprisings. Rural migration swelled the cities, pitifully unprepared for their new populations.

[12] For an old, but balanced, survey see William Cunningham, "Economic Change," *Cambridge Modern History* (8 vols.; Cambridge, England, 1902), I, 493–531.

[13] See Frederic Klemm, *History of Western Technology* (London, 1958); Charles Joseph Singer *et al.*, *History of Technology,* III, "1500 to 1750 A.D." (New York, 1958).

Accompanying the economic outburst, but not necessarily caused by it, political events heralded the emergence of powerful monarchies throughout Europe.[14] Uniquely responding to each nation's needs and dreams, the titan kings of the age dominated their peoples with authoritarian control and dramatic genius. Remarkably coloring their developing world, the overlapping life-spans of Charles V, Francis I, and Henry VIII inevitably induced far-reaching results in European diplomacy and maneuvering. Less domineering in figure, but not less powerful in their personal impact, Leo X and Clement VIII effected political change, not only in terms of their religious position, but in their rank as temporal lords. Warfare was endemic to the period. Until the middle of the century, the campaigns of Charles V involved the entire European community. For every humanist—and with particular poignancy for the gentle Vives—war derisively threw a gauntlet in the face of human nature. Monstrous in its capacity to invade and destroy the lives of innocent and evil alike, war assumed a character at once delirious, bestial, and irrational, arousing fear and repugnance in those who honored reason.

An easy intimacy between religion and life characterized public and private sixteenth-century affairs both before and after the actual rending of the body of the Church. To none of its contemporaries did the Reformation come unannounced. For two centuries honest men had helplessly sought a reconstitution of vital religious life. Even in an eleventh-hour measure, political and

---

[14] See J. W. Allen, *A History of Political Thought in the 16th Century* (reprint: London, 1961); John Neville Figges, *Studies in Political Thought from Gerson to Grotius, 1414–1625* (Cambridge, England, 1931); F. J. C. Hearnshaw, ed., *The Social and Political Ideas of Some Great Thinkers of the Sixteenth and Seventeenth Centuries* (New York, 1926).

personal ambitions had stifled the hopes of the Fifth
Lateran Council (1512–1517).

Before the actual moment of revolt, an undercurrent
of reform had run counter to the common course. Hidden in part, the motivation and practice of the *moderna
devotio* had effectively inspired a strong core of clerics
and laymen.[15] Abuses in monastic living were offset by
the regularity of the Brethren of the Common Life, and
the new orders of clergy such as the Oratorians of Divine
Love and the Theatines. Still, the heart of the body
yearned for broader purification. Reform through one
Council had failed; revolt proposed another alternative.
Was the Reformation necessary? Was a fracturing of the
Church the only means to renewal and regeneration?[16]
In the face of such questions religion assumed a character
of crucial importance to the individual as each Christian
came to answer for himself.

Finally, an intellectual revolution broke over the
times.[17] The arts reflected its structure; education constituted its pivot for action. Every sector of scholarly life
scintillated with change and discovery. Schools in any
culture interpret its present and prophesy its future; not
less so, those of the Renaissance. The new languages of
Greek and Hebrew, joined to Latin, were to enrich
man's expression and enhance his judgment. His training
in rhetorical emphases would oppose scholastic dialectics.
Theology would situate him at the origins of the Gospels
and in the atmosphere of the Church Fathers. He would

[15] See Albert Hyma, *The Christian Renaissance: A History of
the Devotio Moderna* (rev. ed.; Hamden, Conn., 1965); Pierre
Janelle, *The Catholic Reformation* (Milwaukee, Wisc., 1949).

[16] For an answer which sympathetically faces the issue see
Joseph Lortz, *How the Reformation Came* (New York, 1964).

[17] See Denys Hay, "Literature: The Printed Book," in *New
Cambridge Modern History* (New York, 1958), II, 359–386; and
John H. Parry, *The Age of Reconnaissance* (New York, 1963).

challenge interpretations of traditional Scotists. His
changing socioeconomic status argued for a new curriculum and, in circular logic, that education called forth a
new kind of man.[18]

It was this unique Renaissance world down whose
streets Vives walked, in whose universities he taught, in
whose halls and homes he met the men and women so
important in his mental and spiritual formation. Rich
and variegated, contradictory and turbulent, its times
were at once naïve and knowing, eloquent and abrupt,
God-seeking and Church-rejecting. Above all, it was an
era of creativity for humankind caught up in the events
of global exploration, population growth, communication expansion, and religious unrest—all, curiously, with
their parallels in the last third of the twentieth century.

ROADS FROM VALENCIA TO LOUVAIN

Set in the prongs of Eastern Spain's coastline, the city of
Valencia reflects a permanence only lightly shot through
with change. Pre-Christian traders and early-Empire Romans had brought it into being. Moors of the eighth,
ninth, and tenth centuries had settled on it a tradition
of scholarship and a method of juridical legislation
which survived the years.[19] Postmedieval industry and

---

[18] See Denys Hay, "Schools and Universities," in *New Cambridge
Modern History* (New York, 1958), II, 414–437; also the texts already
cited by Lawrence Stone, Joan Simon, and Kenneth Charlton, the
latter's chapters on the Italian influence on English education being keenly perceptive. See also W. H. Woodward, *Vittorino da
Feltre and Other Humanist Educators* (Cambridge, England, 1897;
New York, 1963) which remains a classic study.

[19] Watson, *Luis Vives: El Gran Valencian*, pp. 4 and 9; see also
Castro, *The Structure of Spanish History*, p. 624, regarding Moorish
jurisprudence, and pp. 511–521, regarding the tradition of the
Jewish administration in the government of Spain.

agriculture rarely innovated techniques. For the native
of Valencia in the sixteenth century—or the schoolboy
Latinists of the seventeenth,[20] the wayfarer of the eighteenth,[21] and the visitor of the twentieth[22]—the hills and
the streets, the Water-Gate and the churches, remained
unchanging. Its contours would ever prompt nostalgic
memories.

What spaciousness there is of the market, what a multitude
of sellers and of things exposed for sale! What a smell of
fruit, what variety, what cleanliness, and brightness! . . .
How delightful it is to look up to the Senate House and
fourfold court of the governor of the city, which by now
seems almost to have become the heritage of your family . . .
What buildings! What a glory of a city![23]

A knight's residence came into view on the left as one
descended toward the Quarter of the Cock Tavern.
There Juan Luis Vives was born on March 6, 1492, heir
to a family of old stock, probably rooted in Jewish an-
cestry.[24] The nearby church of St. Agnes, where he was
baptized, stood as only one of innumerable sanctuaries in
a city of Moorish and Christian contrasts. Life in the

---

[20] Vives employed the everyday scenes of a boy's life—such as a
trip around Valencia—in the composition of his famous dialogues
(*Linguae Latinae Exercitatio* [Bruges, 1538]) used for learning
Latin by English and Continental students for almost two cen-
turies. For the English translation, see Foster Watson, *Tudor
School-Boy Life* (London, 1908).

[21] John Ray, *Travels Through the Low Countries* (2 vols.; London, 1738), I, 406–408.

[22] Bart McDowell, "The Changing Face of Old Spain," in *National Geographic*, CXXVII (1965), 291–339.

[23] Watson, *Tudor School-Boy Life*, pp. 205–206. Vives' recollections of his native city remained vibrant when he wrote these
words thirty years after his departure. [Permission of J. M. Dent
& Sons, Ltd.]

[24] Watson, *Tudor School-Boy Life*, p. 201; Castro, *The Structure
of Spanish History*, p. 577.

knightly household, later immortalized in his writings,[25] blended serenely with the Valencian environment. International, regal, and liberal, his native city was to leave a permanent, almost poetic, imprint on his thought and expression.[26]

Although the details of his early schooling have not been preserved, assumptions and legends make credible stopgaps. His early introduction to letters undoubtedly came within the *schola domestica* of his family.[27] A grammar school under "Master Tristany" provided the usual, early formal training in writing and numbers.[28] The Gymnasium of Valencia had been restored by Alexander VI and Ferdinand of Aragon shortly before Vives enrolled in its classes.[29] Twenty years later he was to conjure up its halls in one of his earliest essays:

There is a place at the first entrance into the school which becomes early muddy with the crowd of scholars who have walked through the rain and dust. When you have got over

[25] See Foster Watson, *Vives and the Renaissance Education of Women* (London, 1912), pp. 116–117, his translation of Vives' *De Institutione Foeminae Christianae*, book II, chap. 5. See also p. 131 for a description of the marital love, peace, and respect which existed between the humanist's parents, Luis Vives and Blanche March.

[26] Foster Watson, "The Influence of Valencia and Its Surroundings on the Later Life of Luis Vives as a Philosopher and as a Teacher," in *Aberystwyth Studies*, IX (1927), 27–104. See also Foster Watson, *Vives: On Education* (Cambridge, England, 1913), "Introduction," pp. xvii–cxxi.

[27] See Watson, "The Influence of Valencia," pp. 50–51. Along with basic schooling, a combination of the aims and methods of knightly education traditionally formed a child's early discipline.

[28] Castro, *The Structure of Spanish History*, p. 577, where the author holds that Vives attended a clandestine synagogue with his family until it was discovered by the Inquisition in 1502. Further, "Master Tristany" was later prosecuted for practicing Judaism.

[29] Gregory Manjansius, ed., *Vives Omnia Opera* (8 vols.; Valencia, 1782; Gregg reprint, London, 1964), I, 10–11. See Bonilla, *Luis Vives y la Filosofía*, chap. 1.

this a little, you come upon a high flight of stairs, which lead to decorated bedrooms and halls in which teaching is carried on. It is well-provided with the very best teachers who will come to the place. The forecourt is often somewhat dark, but the arcades are not unpleasant. There is a great cerulean stone under the staircase on which very often packmen, if they have anything new, flock together to sell their books, as if they were condemned to live on the stone.[30]

Within these lecture rooms Vives met Bernard Villanova o Navarro, Daniel Siso, Jerome Amiguet, and the spirit (not the person) of Antonio Lebrijia.

Ironically for one who was to become a leader in a progressive movement, Vives began his academic life in an ultraconservative atmosphere, one which he obediently adopted for his own. In retrospect, Erasmus would one day refer to this period as a time when, still a neophyte scholar, Vives ranked as an outstanding sophist.[31] His tutor, Jerome Amiguet, propounded a thoroughgoing scholasticism, a pedagogy of unregenerate standards, and a stalwart opposition to the hints of an early Renaissance.[32] Antonio Lebrijia, on the other hand, played the role of an Erasmus of Spain, as adept at raising storms and enthusiasms as his noteworthy contemporary.[33] In about 1506 some Valencian scholars suggested the use of Lebrijia's vernacular grammar in the Gymnasium curriculum. Legend persists that Amiguet so influenced his students that the adolescent Vives ardently argued

30 Watson, *Vives: On Education,* p. xlvii. [Courtesy of Cambridge University Press.]

31 Allen *et al., Erasmi Epistolae,* IV, Ep. 1082, lines 46–47. See also De Vocht, *Collegium Trilingue Lovaniense,* I, 232.

32 See Watson, *Vives: On Education,* pp. xlviii–xlix. See also Watson, *Tudor School-Boy Life,* p. x.

33 Watson, *Vives: On Education,* p. xlviii; Allen *et al., Erasmi Epistolae,* II, Ep. 487, line 14; also Henri de Vocht, *Monumenta Humanistica Louveniensis* (Louvain, 1934), p. 444, line 54, for an allusion to Lebrijia.

against the proposed innovation. Thirty years later in his own brilliant *De Disciplinis*,[34] he publicly repudiated his youthful oratory with a warm recommendation for that very text.

By 1510, into his teens and equipped for the advanced techniques of dialectics, he migrated to the University of Paris, probably enrolling at the College of Beauvais.[35] In the ensuing four years his tutors, Gaspar Lax and John Dullaert, groomed him in rigid Aristotelian logic, while he advanced consistently in a reputation for skillful debate.[36] In those formative years at Paris the methods of disputation sank deep roots, as he later wrote:

I received them into my mind when I was impressionable. I applied myself to them with highest zeal. They stick tenaciously. They come up to my mind against my will. They stupify my mind, just as I am reaching forward to better things.[37]

In retrospect, his first full-fledged humanistic essay flayed the early training which had been part of his Parisian discipline. Driving home his point with power and precision, he queried,

Who could tolerate the painter occupying the whole of his life in preparing his brushes and mixing his pigments, or the cobbler spending his life in sharpening his needles, his awls, and his knives, and testing and smearing his threads? If this

[34] Bonilla, *Luis Vives y la Filosofía*, p. 36; Watson, *Tudor School-Boy Life*, p. x. For Vives' commendations, see Watson, *Vives: On Education*, pp. 133, 131, 139, and 162.

[35] Allen *et al.*, *Erasmi Epistolae*, III, Ep. 927, preface; Watson, *Vives: On Education*, p. liv; Bonilla, *Luis Vives y la Filosofía*, pp. 35, 36; Watson, *Luis Vives: El Gran Valencian*, pp. 12–13.

[36] Manjansius, ed., *Vives Omnia Opera*, I, 25–28; Bonilla, *Luis Vives y la Filosofía*, pp. 51–52; Watson, *Luis Vives: El Gran Valencian*, pp. 29–33.

[37] Watson, *Luis Vives: El Gran Valencian*, p. 30, quoting from *In Pseudo-Dialecticos* (Louvain, 1519).

expenditure of time would be intolerable over good logic, what language is adequate to designate that babbling which has corrupted every branch of knowledge?[38]

Typical of scholars of the period he assumed tutorial duties; thus, records report a Peter Garcias de Laloo (who continued at Louvain and Oxford under his tutelage).[39] Perhaps he engaged in actual collegiate teaching, for his first known publication, *Hyginus* (Paris, March 1514), appears to be nothing other than printed lecture notes.

From 1512 on, numerous trips to the Brabant province and its stimulating university town of Louvain separated the young scholar from his ties at the French university. Never robust in health, he may have gone to the Spanish center at Bruges to recuperate in the friendly climate of his countrymen's nurture. He became acquainted with the Valdaura family, Bernard and Clara, who invited him to remain with them, and with the nine-year-old Margaret who was one day to be his wife. At the same time, he was entrusted with the tutoring of James, scion of the distinguished Spanish family de la Poterries. By 1514 master and pupil commuted to Louvain where

---

[38] Watson, *Luis Vives: El Gran Valencian*, p. 31.

[39] For various citations, see Bonilla, *Luis Vives y la Filosofía*, p. 77; and Henri de Vocht, *Literae Virorum Eruditorum ad Franciscum Craneveldium* (Louvain, 1928), Ep. 144, preface. Reference will frequently be made to this series of letters by, and about, Vives and the historical characters with whom he moved. Like Allen's, de Vocht's notes are invaluable. See Vives' *The City of God*, translated by "J. H." [John Healey] (STC 916, London, 1610), book 21, chap. vi, p. 845. This text is the early Stuart translation of Vives' commentaries and redactions of the famous Augustinian work. The reference here is to a dinner at which Peter de Laloo and Vives were present and observed the phenomenon of asbestos for the first time: ". . . we saw also a napkin of it throwne into the middest of a fire, and taken out againe after a while more and white and clean than all the sope in Europe would have made it. . . ."

James matriculated at the university in February and where Vives probably attended lectures in the arts and jurisprudence.[40] In the fall of the same year he opted for permanent residence[41] in Bruges, gateway for trade, diplomacy, and discoveries in life as well as in letters.

Learning now became Vives' irrevocable vocation. At Louvain he was to continue both as tutor and as lecturer. The university consisted of colleges (chiefly of philosophy and theology) and pedagogies (chiefly of grammar and rhetoric). Originally, the latter had been merely preparatory centers for the colleges, often taking residence in boarding houses and inns with such flamboyant names as "Falcon," "Lily," or "Porc." By the 1500's pedagogies had become full-fledged institutes, although they kept their earlier colorful names. Public lectures were given in the *Halles* of the university for all matriculants; private lectures were given in either the colleges or pedagogies for their respective members only. After repeated applications, Vives was licensed in 1520 by the University Council to lecture anywhere in the University even without the usual required degree, such was his repute among the faculties who voted for him.[42]

Tutoring always remained a necessary occupation. In

[40] De Vocht, *Literae Virorum Eruditorum,* Ep. 233, preface.

[41] Watson, *Vives: On Education,* p. xiii; also pp. lxiii–lxvi. The dedication of *De Subventione,* January 6, 1526, supplements this fact, for he refers then to a residence of fourteen years, even if intermittent. A slightly different translation of the entire essay on urban administration of modern social problems can be found in Margaret Sherwood, trans., *Concerning the Poor* (New York, 1917).

[42] For the history of the university see the brilliant four-volume study by de Vocht, already cited. Concerning Vives' license to lecture see de Vocht, *Literae Virorum Eruditorum,* Ep. 2, preface, and Ep. 6; and de Vocht, *Collegium Trilingue Lovaniense,* III, 166. Concerning Vives' nondegreed status, see Henri de Vocht, "Excerpts from the Register of Louvain University from 1485 to 1527," in *English Historical Review,* XXXVII (1922), 89.

1516 he became attached to the eighteen-year-old William of Croy, newly named to the Bishopric of Cambrai that year and the Cardinal-Archbishopric of Toledo the next. For the following five years the lives of the young churchman and the Spanish humanist were intertwined in travel and study at centers in the Lowlands and in France. During the summers of 1519 and 1520, for example, tutor and scholar spent their days at the University of Paris. Vives took the occasion to give a popular series of lectures, at the same time alarming his former faculty with his enthusiastic humanism. However, in January of 1521 the young Cardinal, traveling with Charles V's train through Calais and Cologne to Worms, was killed in a riding accident. The event cast ominous shadows of personal loss and of oncoming penury on the life of his teacher.[43] Until then, Vives had received a regular income as a preceptor. From now on, to support himself he would need to undertake additional lecturing, writing, and tutoring assignments. Never again would his income be secure. The shock of this death, added to the editorial overwork of the moment, apparently induced illness and depression. As he would often do, he withdrew to Bruges for almost half the year in order to convalesce "with my Spanish countrymen."[44]

Of friendship, Vives was to write, "No treasure is more certain than sure friendship, no guard so strong as faithful friends. He takes the sun from out of the world who takes friendship from life." This sun never set on Vives' horizon. His gentle, humble love he proffered alike to the great and the obscure. Letters and essays reflect his fidelity in devotedness, his joy at meeting men attuned

---

43 Allen *et al., Erasmi Epistolae,* III, Ep. 647, preface.

44 Watson, *Vives: On Education,* p. lxxii. He had been received generously by Pedro de Aguirra who cared for him in his illness and even lent him a house for his residence.

to his mind, his generous service and dedication to a friend's concerns.

To illustrate these traits one need only refer to his bonds with Erasmus. Both scholars visited Brussels in 1516 where perhaps they first met. Certainly, their acquaintance must date from at least July of 1517 when Erasmus moved from Antwerp to Louvain in order to initiate Jerome Busleyden's new center for humanistic studies.[45] Undoubtedly a rapt listener at the opening lectures in the new institute, Vives was soon accepted as devoted assistant to and confidant of the great humanist from Rotterdam. Each wrote letters recommending the other as tutor to Ferdinand, the future Emperor. In 1520, Erasmus had commissioned Vives to edit St. Augustine's *City of God* as part of the larger task of emending the writings of the early Church Fathers. For Erasmus, the assignment conferred his highest accolade of respect and admiration on the young Spaniard; for Vives, it deepened his affection for the man more than twenty years his senior whom he would never cease to revere, even in the face of unjust rejection. Employing four manuscripts newly assembled and with the best techniques of the new criticism, Vives produced a valuable edition of the Augustinian classic embedded in rich, humanistic commentaries. Published in 1522 and carrying a dedication to Henry VIII, it reached the book fairs and sellers' stalls by the beginning of the new year. Erasmus wrote grumpily that it was selling poorly; Vives himself had heard of brisk sales.[46] A reserved unfriendliness permeated Eras-

45 See John Jortin, *The Life of Erasmus* (2 vols.; London, 1758–1760), II, 497; also Sinz, "The Elaboration of Vives' Treatises," p. 69. The first volume of de Vocht, *Collegium Trilingue Lovaniense* documents the history of the formative years (1518–1520) of that center of humanism in the Lowlands.

46 Allen *et al., Erasmi Epistolae*, V, Ep. 1531, lines 36–38, for Erasmus' letter; and Ep. 1362, line 40, for Vives'.

mus' letters during a subsequent period, while Vives continued to write to "mi preceptor" as though no offense had been given.

In the meantime, during that first triumphant return to Paris (1519), the erudite of Louvain had been introduced to the brilliantly literate Treasurer of the King, William Budé. Each jubilantly wrote to Erasmus describing their mutual delight at acquaintance. Over the next two years a regular correspondence shuttled between Paris and Louvain.[47] Latter-day historians might name Erasmus, Vives, and Budé to a "Triumvirate of Letters," each with his special jurisdiction of competency.[48] In their own lifetime, however, these three shared an unselfconscious regard for each other's person and gifts, this always in spite of Erasmus' inclination to petulance toward the younger men.

At the same time Thomas More had written to Erasmus, commending the newly published *Somnium* (Louvain, 1520) and the author whom he was yet to meet:

I am ashamed of myself and others with like advantages who take credit for themselves for this or that insignificant booklet, when I see a young man like Vives producing so many well-digested works.[49]

---

[47] Allen *et al.*, *Erasmi Epistolae*, III, Ep. 958, line 112; for Budé's letters to Erasmus, III, Ep. 987, and Ep. 992. For Budé's letters to Vives, IV, Ep. 1023, line 5; also see de Vocht, *Literae Virorum Eruditorum*, Ep. 167, preface, noting letters of August 19, 1519, and January 2, February 2, and April 23, 1520.

[48] Foster Watson, "Juan Luis Vives: A Scholar of the Renaissance, 1492–1540," in *Transactions* of the Royal Society of Literature (new series, I, 1921), pp. 81–102.

[49] Watson, *Luis Vives: El Gran Valencian*, p. 34; Allen *et al.*, *Erasmi Epistolae*, IV, Ep. 1106; J. S. Brewer and James Gairdner, eds., *Letters and Papers Foreign and Domestic* (London, 1875–1896), III, *838* [italic numbers refer to entries, rather than pages]. Also, see de Vocht, *Literae Virorum Eruditorum*, Ep. 115, for the meeting with Vives.

Time and circumstances worked toward their encounter. Friends at Bruges, with common humanistic interests, gathered regularly in the rooms of the Princehof. The Duke of Brabant's great palace, with its courtyard and subsidiary buildings, rose as a city landmark.[50]

The party of Thomas More, accompanying Cardinal Wolsey on embassy from Henry VIII to Charles V, billeted there for a time. On an August afternoon of 1520 Francis Craneveldt, Vives' close friend and More's new acquaintance, introduced the Spanish scholar and the English diplomat. For each, the moment initiated a friendship of lasting and selfless benevolence, later to be tempered in the heat of royal English wrath.

A minuscule income from lectures in the university *Halles* and from his previously published books provided inadequately for Vives' livelihood. In 1522 he turned his Louvain house on Oppendorf Street into a part-time school. Catering chiefly to Spanish boys, he prepared them for their matriculation into the university. Even his garden with its two natural springs, immortalized in the dialogues of his Latin grammar exercises,[51] contributed to the learning environment. A Latin inscription identified the fountains for centuries: *Hic Gemini Fontes, Graecus fluit, atque Latinus.* A modern (1953) archeologist reports that although the Greek fountain had disappeared, the Latin one is still providing the neighborhood with pure, cool, and refreshing water.[52] Men like Honneratus Joannius, Diego Gracian, Peter Mal-

---

[50] Malcolm Letts, *Bruges and Its Past* (London, 1924), pp. 29–30. Facing p. 30 is a sketch of the Princehof from "Sanderus, Flandria Illustrata."

[51] Watson, *Tudor School-Boy Life*, p. 92; and *Linguae Latinae Exercitatio* (Bruges, 1538), in Manjansius, ed., *Vives Omnia Opera*, I, 330.

[52] De Vocht, *Collegium Trilingue Lovaniense*, II, 404.

venda, and Johann Starselius[53] here began their early grammar studies under Vives. Of these, none was more dear to his tutor than Jerome Ruffault, trusted socius after five years of uninterrupted tutelage at Louvain.[54]

The Spaniard also accepted as residents both younger and older scholars from England, tutoring a similar roll of the future great: John Clement, Thomas More's son-in-law, to be exiled under Edward and Elizabeth, Court physician to Mary Tudor; Nicholas Wotton, Tunstall's legal assistant, later to work for Henry's divorce proceedings; William Thale, tutor and companion to Richard Pace, Wolsey's personal ambassador; Antony Barker, Chaplain to Mary Tudor before exile; Nicholas Darryngton, a wandering scholar; and Richard Pate, a future bishop who was to attend the Council of Trent.[55]

[53] De Vocht, *Collegium Trilingue Lovaniense*, II, 404–416. Also, for Honneratus, see Watson, *Tudor School-Boy Life*, pp. 88–92; Manjansius, ed., *Vives Omnia Opera*, I, 105, 120; de Vocht, *Literae Virorum Eruditorum*, Ep. 32, preface. For Gracian, see Allen *et al.*, *Erasmi Epistolae*, VII, Ep. 1913, preface. For Malvenda, see Watson, *Tudor School-Boy Life*, pp. 80–82. For Starselius, see Watson, *Tudor School-Boy Life*, pp. 185–194.

[54] De Vocht, *Literae Virorum Eruditorum*, Ep. 41, preface; Allen *et al.*, *Erasmi Epistolae*, V, Ep. 1303, line 54, and Ep. 1306, lines 45–47; Manjansius, ed., *Vives Omnia Opera*, II, 530–531.

[55] For John Clement, see Allen *et al.*, *Erasmi Epistolae*, II, Ep. 388; III, Ep. 820, line 3; V, Ep. 1256, line 122; and Ep. 1271, lines 115–116; Leslie Stephen and Sidney Lee, eds., *Dictionary of National Biography*, (63 vols.; London, 1885), XI, 33; John Stow, *Annales or a General Chronicle of England* . . . (STC 23340, London, 1631), p. 552; de Vocht, *Collegium Trilingue Lovaniense*, II, 358, 404; de Vocht, *Literae Virorum Eruditorum*, Ep. 154, preface; Foster Watson, *Relaciones de Juan Luis Vives amb els Anglesosmi amb l'Angleterre* (Barcelona, 1918), p. 54; and Anthony à Wood, *Athenae Oxoniensis*, Philip Bliss, ed. (6 vols.; London, 1813), I, cols. 401–402.

For Nicholas Wotton, see Stephen and Lee, eds., *Dictionary of National Biography*, LVIII, 57–61; de Vocht, *Monumenta Humanistica Louveniensis*, p. 4; Nicholas Pocock, *Records of the Reformation* (Oxford, 1870), p. 559; de Vocht, *Literae Virorum Erudi-*

Jerome Busleyden's will had provided financial and legal support[56] for a trilingual institute within the University of Louvain. Under Erasmus' direction, the new college offered instruction in Latin, Greek, and Hebrew. When first proposed, it met with resistance from the combined Faculties of the Arts since it prepared for a critical analysis of texts of the Fathers of the Church, and even of the very Scriptures themselves. To traditional Scholastics everywhere such a program signaled only one outcome: heresy. Reaction was at once violent and vindictive.

Still, not all university professors and deans resisted the cause of the humanists. For one, Adrian Barlandus had guided the young Vives into the rich field of classics

---

torum, Ep. 41, preface; and Manjansius, ed., *Vives Omnia Opera,* II, 530–531.

For William Thale, see Allen *et al., Erasmi Epistolae,* V, Ep. 1256, lines 90 and 91; Ep. 1303, line 51; de Vocht, "Excerpts from the Register of Louvain University," p. 103; and de Vocht, *Collegium Trilingue Lovaniensis,* II, 404.

For Barker, see de Vocht, *Monumenta Humanistica Louveniensis,* p. 11; Manjansius, ed., *Vives Omnia Opera,* II, 287, 303; VII, 141, in which Vives refers to his esteem for Barker because of the latter's devotion to Richard Pate; and J. M. Stone, *The History of Mary I, Queen of England* (London, 1901), p. 203.

For Darryngton, see de Vocht, *Collegium Trilingue Lovaniense,* I, 78; Brewer and Gairdner, eds., *Letters and Papers,* III, *2052, 2204, 2390;* and de Vocht, *Literae Virorum Eruditorum,* Ep. 5, preface.

For Richard Pate, see Frederick Madden, *Privy Purse Expenses of the Princess Mary* (London, 1831), pp. lxxxv–lxxxvi; Thomas Fowler, *History of Corpus Christi College* (Oxford, 1893), pp. 86, 88, 382; Joseph Foster, *Alumni Oxoniensis* (4 vols.; London, 1892), III, 1126; Wood, *Athenae Oxoniensis,* II, cols. 794–795; Brewer and Gairdner, eds., *Letters and Papers,* IV, *4514;* and Stephen and Lee, eds., *Dictionary of National Biography,* XLIV, 10–12.

56 Henri de Vocht, *Jerome Busleyden, His Life and Writings* (Turnhout, 1950). Treating of such specific factors in great detail, this volume began as an introductory essay to de Vocht's four-volume *Collegium Trilingue Lovaniense.*

as early as 1512 or 1513.[57] John Palladanus, entrusted
with the Latin lectures at Louvain, formed Vives' expression in the new rhetoric of the humanists. Adrian of
Utrecht, the future Pope Adrian VI, as professor and
Chancellor of the University, had set his approval in
principle and in practice on the work of the Renaissance
innovators.[58] Scholars, writers, printers, professors, and
public officials forwarded the new learning in spite of
official condemnation by the consistently uncompromising faculty.

The young Spaniard's popularity as a public lecturer
continued to grow. Each year the university Faculty of
Arts sponsored a traditionally vigorous, four-day disputation in mid-December. Called the "Quodlibiticas," discussion could be proposed on any topic whatever, as long
as it was not "turpia, defamatoria, vel ulla ratione offensive."[59] A master chosen by the faculty to preside over the
convocation delivered the original oration, proposed
questions, and led the ensuing debates. The event as-

[57] See innumerable references in the four volumes of de Vocht's
Collegium Trilingue Lovaniense, and in his *Literae Virorum
Eruditorum*, Ep. 62, preface, and Ep. 233, preface. In 1514 Bar-
landus had written, ". . . The diligent Latin scholar, my friend Luis
Vives, of the Spanish nation, has this day through his teaching
aroused the sleeping Latin Muse . . ."; see de Vocht, *Collegium
Trilingue Lovaniense*, I, 233. [My translation.]

[58] Ludwig Pastor, *The History of the Popes* (46 vols.; London,
1906–1953), IX, 34, 48, 85, 86; de Vocht, *Literae Virorum Eruditorum*, Ep. 25, preface, and Ep. 4, p. 55 (purely of tangential interest, this reference is to an illustration of a special swivel armchair
devised by Adrian when he was at Louvain; it permitted the user
to move without the least difficulty, and was requested by the
new Pope from Rome). For the part which Adrian played and the
religious atmosphere generally, see Hubert Jedin, *History of the
Council of Trent* (2 vols.; St. Louis, Mo., 1957–1958), I, 192 ff. and
207.

[59] De Vocht, *Literae Virorum Eruditorum*, Ep. 213, line 30 and
note.

sumed the proportions of an intellectual revelry in which
the entire university joined. Vives' appointment to the
honor in 1522 attracted unparalleled crowds. Taking for
his theme the concept of a jurisprudence which argues on
principle, avoids sophistry, and explains lucidly, he
aroused a fervid, approving response in his audience.[60]
Six months later, at the request of an enthusiastic student
community, he was asked to repeat his commentaries in
the prestigeful University Lecture.[61]

The English Experience

For all Vives' prominence his financial condition wors-
ened. Catherine of Aragon, in spite of the recommendation of Thomas More,[62] had conferred an inadequate,
token pension on him; Henry VIII, to whom Vives had
dedicated his commentaries on *The City of God,* had
only responded with a letter of thanks, instead of the
hoped-for financial settlement. At the same time in
Spain, some unnamed tragedy in Vives' family seemingly
required a personal intervention.[63] The extension of
European wars into neighboring lands hinted at only

[60] De Vocht, *Collegium Trilingue Lovaniense,* II, 211–212; and
III, 520. Also, de Vocht, *Monumenta Humanistica Louveniensis,* pp.
388–389. The speaker appointed in September was apparently unable to fulfill his obligations by December 14. In desperation the
faculty must have applied to Vives, who then had only two days
of preparation. His hurried provision would have explained why
he was unable to give his friends a text of his speech; see de Vocht,
Literae Virorum Eruditorum, Ep. 56, lines 25–34.

[61] De Vocht, *Literae Virorum Eruditorum,* Ep. 56, line 26.

[62] Allen *et al., Erasmi Epistolae,* IV, Ep. 1222, line 17. Prizing his
friendship with More, Vives feared that the advantages he received
might appear to make him seem demanding and mercenary. See
also de Vocht, *Monumenta Humanistica Louveniensis,* p. 2.

[63] De Vocht, *Literae Virorum Eruditorum,* Ep. 32, lines 15–18,
25–29, and preface. Castro, in *The Structure of Spanish History,*
p. 577, quotes Abdan Salazar's suggestion that Vives' father had

further destruction, suggesting good reason for a with-
drawal to peaceableness.[64] Long in the making, Vives'
decision to leave the Lowlands and return to Spain
brought him to immediate action in April of 1523. His
treatise on the education of women, with its dedication
to Catherine, had been completed and he could leave the
manuscript for publication until the following year.[65]
His Spanish students from Oppendorf Street were committed to the benevolent surveillance of the Trilingue.[66]
On May 10 he wrote to both Francis Craneveldt and
Erasmus of his decision to accept the position of lecturer
at the University of Alcala, replacing his youthful target
of derision, Antonio Lebrijia.[67] He was to travel to
Spain via England, thus avoiding the risk of Francis I's
depredation of Flemish shipping, and offered to carry
letters to mutual friends.

On his arrival in London, the bustling Tudor atmosphere pressed almost unbearably on the native Spaniard
who preferred the serenity of a less-compulsive Bruges.
Thomas More had greeted and assisted him, and a daily
call at the Court brought him into sympathetic circles.
Nevertheless his "most distressing, cramped quarters provided no table and hardly a chair, but much noise of inn
and city, where he could not even walk for his health."[68]

---

been under Inquisitorial persecution at this time (and later burned
at the stake) as a Jewish heretic. Manjansius and Watson have
interpreted this unidentified event of sorrow to be the severe illness of the older Vives.

[64] De Vocht, *Literae Virorum Eruditorum*, Ep. 45.

[65] Allen *et al.*, *Erasmi Epistolae*, VI, Ep. 1624, line 61, and VII,
Ep. 1847, line 21.

[66] De Vocht, *Collegium Trilingue Lovaniense*, II, 404.

[67] De Vocht, *Literae Virorum Eruditorum*, Ep. 56, esp. lines 17–20;
Allen *et al.*, *Erasmi Epistolae*, V, Ep. 1362, esp. lines 102–105;
Bonilla, *Luis Vives y la Filosofía*, pp. 153, 630–631.

[68] Manjansius, ed., *Vives Omnia Opera*, VII, 201–202; also de
Vocht, *Monumenta Humanistica Louveniensis*, pp. 6–7.

By August, news from Spain was better, he had moved to another residence, and new friends had offered their assistance. Most importantly, an academic offering came: Cardinal Wolsey named him as Lecturer in Latin, Greek, and Rhetoric at the new Cardinal College, housed temporarily in Oxford's Corpus Christi.[69] The Spanish humanist had hoped for election as a Court Scholar, free for writing and research; still, this appointment to the university provided income and lodging. While his classes of undergraduates proved hardly stimulating, he had time that first quarter for composing six essays and translations. In answer to letters of congratulations from friends in Bruges, he wrote with detachment of the general affection lavished on him and of the joy of moving in the friendly presence of great-minded men, like John Fisher, Charles Mountjoy, Thomas Linacre, and John Claymond.[70]

Long before meeting him, the Bishop of Rochester had expressed his admiration for Vives. Erasmus had written a letter of introduction to the elderly ecclesiastic in 1522 when Vives' plans had first intimated an English visit. When he eventually arrived the following spring, the Spaniard apparently met John Fisher in the large gatherings at Thomas More's.[71] Thomas Linacre, poet and phy-

---

[69] De Vocht, *Literae Virorum Eruditorum*, Ep. 71, lines 25–31. See also Wood, *Athenae Oxoniensis*, I, cols. 141–144; Richard Fiddes, *The Life of Cardinal Wolsey* (London, 1724), p. 248; Thomas Fowler, *Corpus Christi* (Oxford, 1898), pp. 33, 53.

Corpus Christi at Oxford hosted the first generation of English humanists before the educational upheavals of the thirties and forties. From that time on, Corpus Christi at Cambridge entertained a second generation of scholars, perhaps more lasting in historical records because of their Reformation origins and influences.

[70] De Vocht, *Monumenta Humanistica Louveniensis*, p. 10.

[71] Allen *et al.*, *Erasmi Epistolae*, IV, Ep. 1106; V, Ep. 1311, lines

sician, about twenty years Vives' elder, became for him that summer a "dearly loved father." On his part, in his new Latin grammar book, Linacre referred to Vives as "another light arising in letters," thereby choosing to list him with Grocyn, Budé, Erasmus, and More.[72]

Some time in December of that year (1523) Henry and Catherine were returning from Woodstock to the castle at Windsor. To the astonishment of populace and contemporary antiquarians alike, they detoured to Oxford, entered the town, and approached the university quarters to listen to Vives' lectures. An Anglo-Saxon canon traditionally barred the King's entry to the university town, but Henry brushed aside legends and brought his Spanish Queen to hear her confrere. The college basked in Vives' distinction, and willingly paid for the usual gift of gloves for the ladies and for the entertainment demanded by the occasion.[73] Honor piling on honor, Vives was invited for the Christmas holidays to Windsor Castle where Catherine and he delighted in frequent conversations. Forced by ill-health to leave the gaiety of the royal celebrations, he returned to Oxford— and so began the new year of 1524.

Classes resumed, and with them his discouragement at the ineptness of both students and curriculum. Unwill-

---

40–44; de Vocht, *Literae Virorum Eruditorum*, Ep. 80, lines 4–5; Brewer and Gairdner, eds., *Letters and Papers*, III, *838, 2731.*

72 De Vocht, *Literae Virorum Eruditorum*, Ep. 122, line 14; Ep. 80, line 4; Ep. 122, line 13, where Vives notes meeting Linacre; Allen *et al., Erasmi Epistolae,* V, Ep. 1513, line 35. Also, see Henri de Vocht, *Shakespeare Jest Books* (London, 1908), p. 6, for a reference to the relation between Linacre and Vives.

73 De Vocht, *Monumenta Humanistica Louveniensis,* p. 9 and p. 10, the latter quoting from P. S. Allen, "Early Life in Corpus," in *The Pelican Record* (Oxford, 1931). Also, de Vocht, *Literae Virorum Eruditorum,* Ep. 90, lines 19–25, which refer to the subsequent Christmas invitation.

ing to tolerate it longer, he sent to Wolsey his suggestions for a renovated program of studies. For this he received the expressed gratitude of both the Cardinal (who had given his humanist lecturer a free hand in developing the college's studies) and of the University Council itself (who wrote approvingly to Wolsey). At the end of the quarter in mid-April, he returned to Bruges, accompanied by an enthusiastic report of his first English venture.

Of happiest consequence for the rest of his life, he had asked Margaret Valdaura to be his wife.[74] Child of Bernard Valdaura and Clara Cervent, his long-time friends from Bruges, she had grown into the ideal woman such as he had so recently praised in his lyrical essay on the instruction of Christian women. Their marriage was solemnized in the Church of St. Donation by the priest-scholar, John de Fevyn, on May 26, the feast of Corpus Christi. Congratulatory letters arrived throughout the summer. These he answered, sometimes whimsically, always with an element of sober happiness.[75] The couple moved to a larger home on Beghard Street in Bruges, more comfortable than the one on Wool Market, placed at his disposal several years earlier by John Robbyns.[76] Importantly for the current discussion, here that summer he wrote the short treatise which he entitled *Introductio ad Sapientiam.*[77]

With the beginning of the autumn quarter in October of 1524, Vives returned to Oxford for the classes based on

---

[74] De Vocht, *Literae Virorum Eruditorum,* Ep. 102, preface, and lines 7–16; also Ep. 100, 106, 107, 115.

[75] De Vocht, *Literae Virorum Eruditorum,* Ep. 106, 107, especially line 9; also Vives to Erasmus, in Allen *et al., Erasmi Epistolae,* V, Ep. 1455.

[76] De Vocht, *Literae Virorum Eruditorum,* Ep. 112, lines 23–26. This may have been the Valdaura residence (see Ep. 102, preface).

[77] De Vocht, *Literae Virorum Eruditorum,* Ep. 122, lines 20–26.

his renovated curriculum. By comparison with the hundreds at the Trilingue, students here were only a mere handful. The difference stemmed partly from a dissimilarity in over-all faculty membership and objectives, partly from the somewhat extravagant fees at Oxford whereas they were nonexistent at Louvain. In such different circumstances Vives presented his lectures from 1523 to 1526 in intermittent sessions, influencing faculty and students alike. Their names read like a roster of Renaissance immortals, albeit minor: John Claymond, president of Corpus Christi College until 1537; Edward Wotton, student of biology and medicine; Nicholas Udal, playwright and headmaster of Eton; Reginald Pole, advisor to Mary Tudor; John Twynne, schoolmaster and antiquarian; John Heylar, linguist exiled in Henry's later days; and Thomas Lupset, doctor and social philosopher, Vives' earlier visitor at Bruges.

Bleak days in early 1526 presaged the storms of tragedy

---

78 For John Claymond, see Stephen and Lee, eds., *Dictionary of National Biography*, XI, 11; Allen *et al.*, *Erasmi Epistolae*, III, Ep. 990, and V, Ep. 1455, line 21; de Vocht, *Literae Virorum Eruditorum*, Ep. 261, preface; Wood, *Athenae Oxoniensis*, I, cols. 104–106; and de Vocht, *Monumenta Humanistica Louveniensis*, p. 8.

For Edward Wotton, see Stephen and Lee, eds., *Dictionary of National Biography*, LVIII, 48–49; Wood, *Athenae Oxoniensis*, I, cols. 226–227; and Fowler, *History of Corpus Christi College*, pp. 85–86, 88–89, 369–371.

For Nicholas Udal, see Stephen and Lee, eds., *Dictionary of National Biography*, LVIII, 6–9; Wood, *Athenae Oxoniensis*, I, cols. 211–214; and Fowler, *History of Corpus Christi College*, pp. 86–89, 370–371.

For Reginald Pole, specifically as a student of Vives, see Stephen and Lee, eds., *Dictionary of National Biography*, XLVI, 35–46, especially p. 35; and de Vocht, *Collegium Trilingue Lovaniense*, III, 423–424, with special reference to the tutor-student relationship between the humanist and the prelate-to-be.

For John Twynne, see his *De rebus Albionsis Britannicus atque Anglicis* (STC 24407, London, 1590), pp. 6, 41, 131; Stephen and

hovering on the horizon. No sooner had Vives arrived in London than he sensed a general estrangement in political circles stemming from Wolsey's current anti-Spanish policy. Without provocation or warning, he was abruptly dismissed from his lectureship at Oxford. Wolsey grandly attempted to inveigle first Erasmus, then the great Latinist Goclenius, to fill the chair vacated by the Spanish humanist. Once they had refused, the Cardinal allowed the position of Humanities Lecturer to slide into oblivion.[79] By mid-May, with no other course open, Vives returned to Bruges. For the balance of the year he traveled in the Lowlands, insisting to friends that Henry was not to be blamed in the astounding dismissal.

In early April of the following year (1527) he returned to England, determined to discover at first hand his position in the royal circle. The King and Queen remained as hearty as ever in their welcome. In fact, dur-

---

Lee, eds., *Dictionary of National Biography,* LVII, 402–403; and Wood, *Athenae Oxoniensis,* I, cols. 463–465.

For John Heylar, see Stephen and Lee, eds., *Dictionary of National Biography,* XXV, 381–382; Wood, *Athenae Oxoniensis,* I, col. 107; de Vocht, *Monumenta Humanistica Louveniensis,* pp. 599–608 and 14–16, which reproduces a letter written by Heylar when Vives had stayed in London while the Plague raged in Oxford; and de Vocht, *Collegium Trilingue Lovaniense,* III, 423–424, 427.

For Thomas Lupset, see Stephen and Lee, eds., *Dictionary of National Biography,* XXXIV, 285; Fowler, *Corpus Christi,* pp. 87–89; Wood, *Athenae Oxoniensis,* I, col. 28, 69–72; Allen *et al.,* I, Ep. 270, line 60; V, Ep. 1362, line 44; and de Vocht, *Literae Virorum Eruditorum,* Ep. 169, line 1. For Lupset's writings see *Thomas Lupset's Workes* (STC 16932, London, 1546).

79 De Vocht, *Literae Virorum Eruditorum,* Ep. 156, preface; Ep. 175, line 56; Ep. 178, line 6; Ep. 182, lines 17–23; Ep. 172, preface; Allen *et al., Erasmi Epistolae,* VI, Ep. 1665, line 20; Ep. 1682, line 2; Ep. 1697, lines 94–98; and Watson, *Vives and the Renaissance Education of Women,* pp. 16–18.

ing May, Henry and he worked closely on a "joint" answer—destined never to be published—to Luther's letter
of September 1, 1525.[80] When Vives asked to return to
Bruges because of illness in his family, Henry magnani-
mously granted the travel permit but only on condition
that the humanist would assume the Latin tutorials of
Mary Tudor in October.

By the fall, the English king's interests had shifted to
matters other than Latin grammar or German theology.
Diplomatic intrigue had smoldered throughout the summer. With the increased threat of war, the spreading
religious convulsions, and the disheartening news of
Erasmus' rejection again by the great universities, the
world situation generally seemed impossible of recovery
without open conflagration. Vives found himself writing
that there was no hope even for a new day—a black mood,
indeed, for one usually optimistic.[81] Still, his word having
been given, he returned to England, journeyed to Green-
wich, and began his Latin lessons with the royal pupil.
Catherine was there as well, like the entire Court looking
to Vives as her defender in the face of the King's unbe-
lievable proposal for "divorce."

Wolsey now began a series of desperate measures. No
matter the means, he must accumulate compromising
evidence against Catherine; Vives, as a fellow-country-
man, offered a logical opening for the offensive. Late that
year, perhaps at the beginning of 1528, the Cardinal himself interrogated his former lecturer concerning Cath-

---

[80] De Vocht, *Literae Virorum Eruditorum*, Ep. 235, lines 17–20;
Ep. 241, preface; Ep. 261, preface; Ep. 237; Brewer and Gairdner
eds., *Letters and Papers*, IV, 2446; Watson, *Relaciones de Juan
Luis Vives*, pp. 272–273; Allen *et al.*, *Erasmi Epistolae*, VII, Ep.
1836; and Mandell Creighton, *Cardinal Wolsey* (London, 1888), pp.
130, 150–151.

[81] De Vocht, *Literae Virorum Eruditorum*, Ep. 246.

erine's confidences shared over the years.[82] Every letter the Spaniard wrote, every place he visited, every person he saw was kept under supervision. By early February Wolsey demanded more, a written statement of Vives' position concerning the annulment proceedings. From his expectedly uncompromising support of Catherine, only one consequence could issue. Wolsey immediately placed the writer under total house arrest. Cited with him was Inigio de Mendoza, current Imperial Ambassador, to whom the Spanish humanist had appealed at the onset of the crisis. From February 25, for at least thirty-eight days, the two men had no visitors and no correspondence, except such as had been intercepted by Wolsey's men. By word and gesture Henry openly approved of the Cardinal's handling of the case.

Suddenly, on the specific stipulation that he would never again return to England, Vives was released in the first week of April. Four traveling days from London to the Lowlands brought a disillusioned, yet typically loyal, Spanish humanist home to Bruges. Ignoring popular curiosity, he rarely referred to the event of his imprisonment except to his closest friends, and then only with cautious discretion. Officially, the royal pensions continued, at least on the books; however, long before his name was withdrawn from the lists, he had stopped receiving the stipends regularly.

In the autumn of that year (1528) the Papal Court had assembled in London for the hearing of evidence regarding the annulment once granted to Henry and Catherine. With a farcical attempt at justice, the King conceded to Catherine not the Spanish lawyers she had requested, but two advocates from Flanders and, amaz-

82 De Vocht, *Literae Virorum Eruditorum,* Ep. 261; Ep. 251, line 5; Ep. 254, line 9.

ingly, Juan Luis Vives. The arrival of the three ap-
pointees in England in mid-November was carefully observed and recorded.[83] Vives immediately advised the
beleaguered Queen to have no part in the charade of so-
called legal equity. With a desperation stemming at once
from stubbornness and loneliness, she summarily dismissed her would-be defender and sent him forlornly
back to the Continent. Along with the King's pension,
the Queen's stipend now ended. Still, Catherine's policy
in the succeeding unhappy months demonstrated a strategy of "passive resistance," much as Vives had suggested.
Unaware of her future decision, he continued to write
of her only in terms completely innocent of grudge or
condemnation.[84]

DESCENT TOWARD DEATH

For the next ten years the details of Vives' life lose their
sharpness. He often traveled to Louvain, on at least one
occasion presenting a series of lectures which recalled the
wildly popular days of the Quodlibiticas.[85] He continued
to make last-ditch attempts at turning Henry from the
divorce. On the one hand, he wrote directly to the King
arguments based on the "memoir" Wolsey had demanded of him. On the other, he apparently circulated
several anonymous tracts condemning the King's action.

[83] Brewer and Gairdner, eds., *Letters and Papers*, IV, 4875,
4938–4939, 4943–4946; see also Bonilla, *Luis Vives y la Filosofia*,
p. 215.

[84] As in his newly published *De Offici Maritii*, quoted in Watson,
Vives: On Education, p. lxxxi. To summarize Vives' residence
in England, the six sojourns include: May 1523 to April 1524,
October 1524 to May 1525, February 1526 to May 1526, April 152
to June 1527, October 1527 to April 1528, and November 1528.

[85] De Vocht, *Collegium Trilingue Lovaniense*, II, 615, 616; III,
77.

both from the point of view of religion and of reason.[86]
Angered beyond replying, Henry wrathfully ordered the
Spaniard's name formally struck from the pension books
—and the last link between earlier friends was finally
broken.

Inadequate sales of his books, and the nonpayment of
a promised Imperial pension, combined to bring him to
penury and probably to imprisonment.[87] Illness had
plagued him for years, but now it reached its full fury.
He suffered from intense pain in his head and eyes. Gout
had spread through his hands, knees, and arms, up into
his shoulders.[88] In the famous dialogues he could still af-
ford to smile wanly about his affliction:

MASTER. But what is our Vives doing?
NEP. They say he is training as an athlete, yet not by
athletics.
MASTER. What is the meaning of that?
NEP. He is always wrestling, but not bravely enough.

---

[86] Brewer and Gairdner, eds., *Letters and Papers*, V, *46;* de
Vocht, *Literae Virorum Eruditorum*, Ep. 261, preface; Bonilla,
Luis Vives y la Filosofía, pp. 648, 786. See document, "Non
Esse . . .," in de Vocht, *Monumenta Humanistica Louveniensis*, p.
37. De Vocht suggests that internal evidence confirms Vives' author-
ship. The government apparently judged the same; thus, when
Bishop Fisher was interrogated in the Tower four years later, he
was accused of inciting Vives' arguments, as in *Letters and Papers*,
VIII, *859.*

[87] De Vocht, *Monumenta Humanistica Louveniensis*, p. 42; see
also P. S. Allen, *Age of Erasmus* (Oxford, 1914), p. 306.

[88] Several references to his health appear through the years. In
1522, see Allen *et al.*, *Erasmi Epistolae*, IV, Ep. 1222, line 12; V,
Ep. 1306, lines 8–12, 17–19; and de Vocht, *Literae Virorum Eruditorum*, Ep. 8, lines 7 and 33; Ep. 13, lines 5 and 53–58. In 1523,
see de Vocht, *Literae Virorum Eruditorum*, Ep. 80. In 1524, *ibid.*,
Ep. 90, line 40; in 1525, Ep. 166, line 21; Ep. 136, lines 36–52;
in 1527, Ep. 266, line 18; Ep. 248, lines 9–19. He was also affected
by the heat: see *Literae Virorum Eruditorum*, Ep. 112, line 45; Ep.
53, line 17; Ep. 159, line 21.

MASTER.   With whom?
NEP.   With his gout.
MASTER.   O mournful wrestler, which first of all attacks the feet.
USHER.   Nay, rather cruel victor, which fetters the whole body.[89]

However, the more violently he suffered from physical and psychological blows, the more richly and profusely he wrote. These were the years of the great *De Disciplinis*, the *De Causis Corruptarum Artium*, and *De Ratione Docendi*.[90] These were the years of the *Preces et Meditationes*; the *Praeparatio Animi*, his thoughtful meditations on prayer; of *De Concordia et Discordia*, and of *De Pacificatione*, typical humanistic treatises on the value of peace and the savagery of war; of *De Anima*, and *Linguae Latinae Exercitatio*, that monumental study of the theory and principles of psychology, and its application in the study of language; and finally his theological work, *De Veritate Fidei*, which was edited posthumously by Francis Craneveldt at the insistence of Margaret Valdaura.

Throughout the thirties he made short trips to Ghent, Mechlin, and Brussels. At one time, in 1536, he apparently remained in Paris for about six months. Eventually, the tardy pension arrived from Charles V, and another from John III, King of Portugal.[91] These, together with

89 Watson, *Tudor School-Boy Life*, p. 24.

90 See Sinz, "The Elaboration of Vives' Treatises," for the history of these texts: he traces their origin from 1525 through publication, showing Vives' adamant adherence to a "new" education. In order to promote sales, Vives gave two Orations that year on the subject of education. After this he seemed to avoid his friends in chagrin at seeming so "mercenary." See Allen *et al., Erasmi Epistolae*, VIII, Ep. 2352, lines 345–348 and 373–376; also de Vocht, *Collegium Trilingue Lovaniense*, II, 616, and III, 25.

91 De Vocht, *Monumenta Humanistica Louveniensis*, p. 430. Vives' friends (like Rodrigo Manrique) were active on his behalf.

fees in 1537 and 1538 from tutorial duties to Menci de Mendoza in Breda, eased the Spanish humanist's financial disability during his last years.

Correspondence reflected his continuing fidelity to friends. For several years, no letters had been exchanged with Erasmus. In 1529 the latter had published a second edition of *The City of God,* with corrections from a newly discovered manuscript, but completely bare of Vives' notes and introduction.[92] Abruptly on Christmas Eve of 1533, perhaps at the instigation of mutual friends, Erasmus wrote a note protesting his undying loyalty, chagrined at being suspected of coldness and disaffection.[93] In spite of this sudden reversal of the older man's expressed feelings, Vives' return letter quickly reasserted the same manly fondness for his mentor which had been his from the first. The suppression of his work had never caused him displeasure, as he had said once before. The moment for Erasmus' statement in the matter of the divorce in England had passed. Rather, they should support each other in a greater grief over the peril of John Fisher and Thomas More whom they both loved.[94]

[92] Allen *et al., Erasmi Epistolae,* IV, Ep. 1222, preface and contents. See also V, Ep. 1309, for a lengthy preface regarding the history of this work; and Foster Watson, "J. L. Vives and St. Augustine's *Civitas Dei,*" in *Church Quarterly Review,* LXXXVI (1913), 127–151.

[93] Eramus' letter is not extant, although Vives reply is: see Allen *et al., Erasmi Epistolae,* VII, Ep. 2932.

[94] For Vives' earlier assurance of good will, see Allen *et al., Erasmi Epistolae,* VII, Ep. 2208, line 20, and Ep. 2061, lines 73–76. Concerning the divorce, see Vives' request for a strong reprimand, VI, Ep. 1850, line 8, and Erasmus' answer, VII, Ep. 2040. See Henri de Vocht, *Acta Thomae Mori* (Louvain, 1947), pp. 75–85, which is an answer to studies suggesting that the respect and devotion between Erasmus and More had never been a permanent disposition; see also Margaret Philips, *Erasmus and the Northern Renaissance* (New York, 1965).

They should grieve together over the incredible calamities which had overtaken their world. In the presence of sorrow, their own private tragedy, their estrangement, would be healed.

Still, sadness had not reached its nadir. The mourning for More and Fisher in 1535 gave way the following year to wordless anguish at the death, in January, of the courageous Queen from Aragon; then in July (too swiftly) of Erasmus, the dear teacher from other years, the *mi amice* of Louvain and Bruges.

Writing and study, tutoring and prayer filled four successive years, themselves dark with universal apprehension. Then at Bruges on May 6, 1540, Juan Luis Vives departed from a life which he had always loved intensely, and yet had held lightly for the promise of a richer, eternal existence. There in the city of his adoption and at the altar of his wedding, the maimed and disabled body was interred in the St. Joseph Chapel, Church of St. Donatian. Keeping witness to the end stood his cherished wife, Margaret, and the ever faithful familiars, Francis Craneveldt, John de Fevyn, and Mark Laurin. Left to mourn were the friends and fellow-scholars of Bruges, Louvain, Antwerp, Paris, London, and Oxford—indeed, all students, past and present, whom he would introduce to wisdom, that prize of the Renaissance generation.

A RENAISSANCE TEXTBOOK IN ITS TUDOR MILIEU

Students of educational or intellectual history know the *Introductio ad Sapientiam* more through description than through experience. On secondary evidence alone, modern commentators have elevated Juan Luis Vives' little book to the rank of classic in pedagogy and philosophy. One may cynically observe that such a distinction too often means canonization by the professional community and rejection by the students for whom it was intended. Admittedly, the work does not reflect twentieth-century procedures in learning. Yet its basic principles—of growth in courtesy, charity, practical wisdom, and intellectual appreciations—continue germane to modern education and the needs of contemporary society.

Its role in the sixteenth century, and for decades beyond, stemmed from an intrinsic value perceived consciously or felt intuitively by English and Continental educators. As a device for training in grammatical skills, the *Introductio* ranked with the Renaissance restorations of admired Greeks and Romans, or with the linguistic prodigies of Erasmus and Budé. As a wellspring of ethical precepts, it provided persuasive moralistic advice for upright living. In an ambivalent era of religious commitment and controversy, it satisfied a universal desire for theological inspiration. Finally, it reflected the social conditions and aspirations of an emerging middle class by being absorbed into the mental and emotional preparation of "gentlemen" in their grammar schools. When these objectives waned, the popularity and functional usefulness of the *Introductio* waned. But while they formed the core of European and English enthusiasms, the *Introductio* precisely reflected its own era.

The Tudor curriculum both prepared for, and then supported, the brilliance of Elizabethan letters and life. A new layman, a new gentleman,[95] walked upon the

95 Studies on this phenomenon, already prolific, have become more tantalizing with their new insights from the behavioral and

nation's stage. Principles of humanism, once the private
prerogative of individuals within wealthy and restricted
circles, extended through education to a larger public.
Programs of study embraced the masters of antiquity,
whether the theory of teaching followed the method of
St. Paul's or its pedagogical rival, Eton.[96] "Modern"
authors entered upon the sacrosanct ground of classicism
only by concession, this granted universally to Erasmus,
Corderius, and Vives.[97]

The little book of moral axioms from Vives' pen
reached the English public in the late autumn of the
year of his death, 1540, through Richard Morison's
translation.[98] At least by 1561, if not earlier, the *Introduc-*

---

social sciences: G. R. Elton, *England under the Tudors* (New York,
1954), specifically p. 431. For a collection of sixteenth-century
sources enriched by twentieth-century commentaries, see Ruth
Kelso, *Doctrine of the English Gentleman in the Sixteenth Century*
(Urbana, Ill., 1929).

[96] For the movement of humanism to the lower echelons see
Lewis Spitz, *The Religious Renaissance of the German Humanists*
(Cambridge, Mass., 1963), p. 292. For a very detailed account of the
growth and development of these two English systems, see T. W.
Baldwin, *William Shakspere's Small Latine and Lesse Greeke*
(2 vols.; Urbana, Ill., 1944), I, especially chaps. 14–19.

[97] J. Howard Brown, *Elizabethan Schooldays* (Oxford, 1933), p.
76, refers to isolated instances of works by Mantuan, Palingenius,
Sedulis, and George Buchanan, contrasting with the universal use
of texts by the acknowledged leaders of humanistic thought.

[98] That same year Berthelet also published another edition of
Richard Hyrde's translation of *The Instruction of Christian
Women*. One suspects a businessman's shrewd capitalizing on the
current interest in Vives' works, highlighted by news of the passing
of the great humanist.

For the life of Richard Morison, see, among others, Stephen and
Lee, eds., *Dictionary of National Biography*, XXXIX, 60–61; W. G.
Zeeveld, "Richard Moryson, Official Apologist for Henry VIII," in
P.M.L.A., LV (1940), 406–425; Wasey Sterry, *The Eton College
Register, 1441–1695* (Eton, 1943), p. 238; C. R. Baskerville, "Sir
Richard Morison as the Author of Two Anonymous Tracts on

tion to Wysdome had become part of the English school curriculum. Then, for one hundred years and more, it functioned within the broad stream of English pedagogy. Vives' dialogues became the far more popular work, yet the *Satellitiae* and the *Introductio* found a place in the course requirements of both royal tutorials and of the numerous grammar schools surfacing in the flood of educational involvement.[99] Alexander Nowel, dean of St. Paul's and later author of the important Elizabethan catechism, owned a Latin edition of the *Introductio*; Edward VI quoted sayings from the *Satellitiae* in his schoolboy letters. Master Peter Young, preceptor of the future James I, catalogued a handsomely bound gift copy of the *Introduction* when the boy would have been about

---

Sedition," in *Library*, New Series, XVII (1937), 83–87; Thomas Fuller, *The History of the Worthies of England* (3 vols.; London, 1860), I, 508–509. Morison himself gives hints of his dependence on patrons in the dedication of his translation of the *Introductio ad Sapientiam* to Thomas Cromwell's son and also in *The Strategems, Sleghtes and Policies of Warre* . . . (STC 11402, London, 1539). See also many references in Brewer and Gairdner, eds., *Letters and Papers*, IX, *101–103*, X, *372, 417–419, 465, 660, 801, 961, 970;* XI, *328, 513;* XIV, *538*.

For Gregory Cromwell to whom Morison dedicated his work, see Thomas Merriman, *Life and Letters of Thomas Cromwell* (2 vols.; Oxford, 1902), I, *53;* see also Brewer and Gairdner, eds., *Letters and Papers*, IV, *4560, 4837, 4916,* and others for the tutor Cheking's reports on the boy's ineptness in studies.

[99] See Lawrence Stone, *The Crisis of the Aristocracy*, for an analysis of this. A. F. Leach in his books on the history of Tudor education and in his various Victoria County History essays did yeoman work in this research, as *English Schools at the Reformation, 1546–8* (Westminster, 1896) and *Educational Charters and Documents* (Cambridge, England, 1911). Joan Simon, in her massive recent volume, attacks the logic of his conclusions. For her same discussion in shorter essays, see *British Journal of Educational Studies*, III (1955), 128–143; IV (1956), 32–48; and XII (1964), 41–50. See also, "The Reformation and English Education," in *Past and Present*, XI (1957), 48–65.

ten or eleven years of age, and ready for First Form subjects.[100]

Two rival systems of teaching grammar had emerged in the early sixteenth century. As educational pace-setters, Eton, Westminster, and St. Paul's each influenced a further series of preparatory institutions. Their choice of "vulgars"—material to be translated from English to Latin—illustrates a typical difference between the two trends. The St. Paul's system normally required the Bishops' version of the Psalms, Proverbs, and Ecclesiasticus, as can be shown in the grammar school at Stratford-on-Avon. On the other hand, for at least a half-century the Eton system successfully employed moralistic, non-Biblical sources and eventually stimulated a wide use of the writings of the French Corderius, the international Erasmus, and specifically the dialogues and "introductions" of the Spanish Vives. Thus, at the Stratford school, Shakespeare must have turned Biblical passages from English to Latin. Still, as a concession to the Etonian influence, he evidently used Vives' *Satellitiae* in the reverse process of working from Latin to English, since substantial influences can be discovered in the *Merchant of Venice, Corialanus, Twelfth Night, The Tempest, Love's Labour's Lost,* and *Hamlet.*[101]

Evidence of the use of the *Introduction to Wysdome* clearly exists in at least five Tudor schools which, coin-

---

[100] For Nowel, see Baldwin, *William Shakspere's Small Latine,* I, 174. For Edward, see Brewer and Gairdner, eds., *Letters and Papers,* XXI, *61, 1036, 1148;* also quoted in John Nichols, ed., *Literary Remains of King Edward Sixth* (London, 1857). For James I, see Baldwin, *op. cit.,* I, 532.

[101] Baldwin, *William Shakspere's Small Latine,* I, 689, 690, 744; II, p. 544. Also, see T. W. Baldwin, *William Shakespere's Petty School* (Urbana, Ill., 1943), pp. 147–149, and Watson, *Tudor School-Boy Life,* pp. 67, 95, 130, 123.

cidentally, followed the Eton system.[102] Westminster employed it in the revised curriculum of 1561. Although it is not indicated by name, "Vives" and "Vives' dialogues" are each listed for two days of reading. Since it would have been contrary to every current practice to have four days of construing on the same text, and since the dialogues are specified, the other selection must have been the *Introduction*. Sir Philip Sydney was using an adapted version at Shrewsbury Grammar School by 1565, according to an accounting of his allowance.[103] Schools at Norwich and Rivington followed with its use about the same time. Gabriel Goodman, dean of Westminster and close friend of William Burleigh, instituted its use as a text for the First Form in his new school at Ruthin, North Wales, in 1574.[104] While Latin editions could have been obtained from printers abroad, two such editions issued from Aberdeen in 1623 and from Cambridge in 1643.

Aside from his texts designed for students, Vives' influence extended to the schools through his pedagogical writings, especially in the twenty books of the *De Disciplinis*. The work appeared in Antwerp in 1531, the same year as the London edition of Thomas Elyot's *The Boke Named the Governour*. For this reason—or perhaps because philosophizing on education had peaked[105] and the new trend would turn toward practicality and appli-

[102] Baldwin, *William Shakspere's Small Latine*, I, 366; and Foster Watson, *English Schools to 1660: Their Curriculum and Practice* (Cambridge, England, 1908), pp. 332–333.

[103] Baldwin, *William Shakspere's Small Latine*, I, 366.

[104] See Appendix F of Richard Newcome, *A Memoir of Gabriel Goodman with Some Account of Ruthin School* (Ruthin, 1825); also Lewis Stanley Knight, *Welsh Independent Grammar Schools to 1600* (Newtown, 1926).

[105] See Sinz, "The Elaboration of Vives' Treatises on the Arts," pp. 68–90.

cation—a contemporary translation was not produced. Nevertheless, the theoretical propositions of the book, its radical approaches to reading, history, counseling, school planning, and linguistics, exerted pressures both directly and indirectly.[106]

The first is obvious; the second was more far-reaching. Renaissance authors shared a concept of "borrowing" another's works which today would be defined as plagiarism.[107] Outright pilfering was never justified, but imitation of technique and of expression—even with the same general concepts—became an admired performance. Thus, Vives' pedagogical analyses found in the works of succeeding English theoreticians are present not through malicious thievery but, on the contrary, through honorable imitation. Roger Ascham and Richard Mulcaster in the 1570's illustrate the situation most pointedly, while John Milton concludes a century's dependence on Vives' originality. The Continental writings of Johann Sturm and Johann Comenius qualify for the same observation concerning influence and imitation, as they themselves and their works testify.[108]

For whom did Vives write the *Introductio ad Sapientiam*? In his letter to Francis Craneveldt, dated from Oxford in January 1525, he referred to his newly pub-

---

106 For a direct reference see Richard Mulcaster, *Positions*, Robert Herrick Quick, ed. (London, 1888), p. 259.

107 See Harold Ogden White, *Plagiarism and Imitation during the English Renaissance* (Cambridge, England, 1935); see also Flora Ross Amos, *Early Theories of Translation* (New York, 1920), pp. 81–132.

108 As in S. S. Laurie, *Life and Works of Comenius* (Boston, n.d.) wherein the author points out that Comenius himself referred to his first impulses toward realism as originating in his reading of Vives. An example of imitation: Ascham absorbed Vives' frequent references to the pupils' growth from within and of the teacher's duty to stimulate inner direction; the English writer has received more credit than the Spanish innovator.

lished work as one designed "for young boys or even for adolescents."[109] Evidently from the context he excluded little children and mature adults, the two definitional extremes of his "puer" and "adulescens," indicating rather those of an age just previous to university studies. Evidence rises from his own experiences. By 1524 when the book was published, he had been teaching in the *Halles* of the University at Louvain for at least five years. He had been lecturing at Oxford's Corpus Christi College from September of the previous academic year. From his earliest years of tutoring, he had been accepting only pupils within the range of adolescent years. Young men, such as the students at the Trilingue and at Oxford, the boarders at Oppendorf Street, and the private pupils at Bruges, were evidently in mind as he wrote. In fact, the lines of the *Introductio* read so conversationally that one suspects the work to have grown out of his counseling after class hours.

Further, acquiring such moral precepts followed the classical notion of education for young adults, as popularized by the rejuvenated study of Quintilian's *Institutes*. In such a spirit Thomas Elyot considered students at seventeen to be at the most appropriate age for the study of moral philosophy.[110] Theoretically, then, the *Introductio* was intended for an age level of the English Sixth Form; historically, however, it functioned over the years in the First Form, never higher than the Second, for boys ten or twelve years of age, if not younger.

Vives' *Introductio* lists the specifics of hygiene, as Erasmus' popular *De Civilitate* does; it has the specifics of behavior toward others, as the anonymous *Institution*

---

[109] De Vocht, *Literae Virorum Eruditorum*, Ep. 136, lines 20–34, especially, 30–32.

[110] Thomas Elyot, *The Book Named the Governour*, Henry H. S. Croft, ed. (2 vols.; London, 1883), I, 91.

of a Gentleman does.[111] However, it goes beyond both in its unique analysis and counsels concerning human actions which are rational and ultimate. For these young men he would write at times almost poetically of the satisfactions of the intellectual life, of the excellence of friendship, of the obligations of truth and charity. Perhaps at first confused by nonmeaningful advice, First Formers in English grammar schools nevertheless grew into the large ideas cut by the author for older minds than theirs. Indeed, with delayed approval, they required for their own children the same introductory text for grammar.

The *Introductio ad Sapientiam* first appeared in the late fall of 1524 in Louvain, apparently issued by Peter Martens,[112] son of the great Brabant printer, Thierry Martens. Jerome Ruffault, Vives' young friend and student, had remained in the university town to oversee the printing while his preceptor went to England for the winter quarter at Corpus Christi. As proofreader of text and collator of pages, Ruffault would have performed functions often assumed by a writer's assistant.[113] Actually, as the title page showed, the little work was added as a companion-piece to Vives' two works published in the previous year, the *Satellitiae* and the two *Epistolae* on studies for boys.[114]

[111] Erasmus' *De Civilitate Morum Puerilium per Des Erasmum Roterodamum* . . . (STC 10467, London, 1532), and the anonymous *Institution of a Gentleman* (STC 14105, London, 1555).

[112] Vives refers to the publishers in de Vocht, *Literae Virorum Eruditorum,* Ep. 136, lines 126–134. See also André F. Iseghem, *Biographie de Thierry Martens D'Alost* (Alost, 1856), and M. J. Gard, *Recherches . . . sur la vie et les éditions de Thierry Martens* (Alost, 1845).

[113] De Vocht, *Literae Virorum Eruditorum,* Ep. 144, line 30; Ep. 122, line 22.

[114] Gard, *Recherches . . . de Thierry Martens,* seems to have had a first edition copy with him in his description, "Octavo with-

Reissues began immediately. In the same year as the Martens imprint a separate edition appeared in Strasbourg, followed by reprints in Bruges, Paris, Antwerp, another in Louvain, two in Basle, and one in Leipzig, all in Vives' lifetime. After that, thirty-five further editions appeared in Latin up to 1732; four editions in French between 1548 and 1553; one in German in 1545; fifteen in Spanish between 1544 and 1886; one in Spanish in Mexico City in 1560; and seven known printings in English between 1540 and the 1570's. Thus, the editions amount to at least seventy-six, although the total must be considered open to continuing correction as new reprints are made or old editions are discovered.

As a textbook for Tudor schools, the *Introduction to Wysdome* in an ordinary edition would have run to 1250 copies. In extraordinary cases, an edition of texts could go as high as 10,000, as with Lily's grammar which had been declared a required version in all schools. To protect the market for printers, the Stationers' Company's rules required a complete resetting of any reissues, thus accounting for the many, but minute, differences in spelling and pagination found in surviving copies. For this reason schoolbooks ranked as one of "the most lucrative of publishing properties."[115]

School texts appeared as paper-covered pamphlets,[116] most literally "paper-back editions," with bindings ordi-

---

out pagination, with catchwords and signatures printed in Roman characters, with large engraved initials, and with arabic numbers in the margin." The latter numeration would have referred to the individual "introductions" which were enumerated in the Latin editions, although Morison dropped them in his translation.

[115] Edward Arber, ed., *A Transcript of the Registers of the Company of Stationers of London, 1554–1640* A.D. (5 vols.; Birmingham, England, 1894), II, 23.

[116] Brown, *Elizabethan Schooldays,* p. 52.

narily an added expense not consistently assumed by money-strapped school boys. Surviving copies in twentieth-century libraries show the dog-eared, rumpled, scribbled condition associated with reluctant learners in all ages.[117] Perhaps other editions of Richard Morison's translation of the *Introductio* had been printed but, under the prevailing circumstances, proved too fragile to survive the manhandling of restless First or Second Formers throughout England and Wales.

THE RENAISSANCE THEMES OF VIVES

Some depths of the northern Renaissance may best be plumbed in degrees of commitment to religion. In time, theological originality and initiative were to founder disastrously on polemics. An eighteenth-century deist rationalism would supplant religious faith. Science, stripped clean of all ends and objectives except its own existence and progress, would fashion another era. But in its early decades Protestant and Catholic sixteenth-century religion called forth new expressions of the arts and sciences in joyous, reckless abundance.

Sensitivity to this fact illumines the analysis of any Renaissance mind, and none more than that of Juan Luis Vives. The whole world had been fit subject for his pen. For him all life came to a focus in God and

117 For example, a copy of the 1532 edition of Erasmus' *De Civilitate* is marked with scratches, blots, hands, comments, exclamation points, and letters repeated (with a signature of "Thomas Bentley" on page F.D. added from another era). The Tudor script (which predominates) also notes a date and place, "Canterbury, 1571." In 1596 a certain John Beale "of the Citty of Chichester in the County of Sussex" left his assignment reminders on five pages through his *Esop,* in print, manuscript, and secretary penmanship. On one page he practiced the whole alphabet in the three hands. Both books were examined at the Huntington Library.

His revelation to the world through Christ His Son. While he could write meticulously on such diverse subjects as ancient drama and contemporary domestic economy, he found in their ultimate objectives a unifying element of existence. His texts in psychology and in the theory of education, for example, broadly embody a purposive organicism.[118] This was the laurel which he and his fellow-humanists claimed for themselves—orderly cohesion structured in hierarchical unity.

The *Introductio ad Sapientiam* resembles wax which has received the impress of a signet. Not designed as a treatise on physiology, psychology, philosophy, or theology, nevertheless its lines are so informed by those sciences that to read the *Introductio* is to read the obverse of their theses. It stands not quite midway between the richly humanistic *City of God* commentaries of 1522 and the highly professional *De Disciplinis* of 1531. Its lines reflect the practicalities of ten years of teaching, as well as latent theories yet to be elaborated.

Penetrating its every phrase is a profound awareness of man as creature redeemed by Christ, eternally destined for a freely chosen future. Still, the book is not a pious collection of precepts on "how to be good." Contrary to some opinion, it does not bear legitimate comparison to the *Imitation of Christ*.[119] Written in the

[118] Vives, *The City of God,* Book I, chap. 30, p. 47; Book II, chap. 7, p. 63; *De Subventione Pauperum,* published by Hubert de Crooc (Bruges, 1526), as in Manjansius, ed., *Vives Omnia Opera,* IV, 420–494; see Sherwood, *Concerning the Poor,* for a translation into English. *De Anima* (Basle, 1538), as in *Vives Omnia Opera,* II, 299–520; *De Disciplinis* (Antwerp, 1531), as in *Vives Omnia Opera,* VI, 3–437, consisting of *De Corruptarum Artis,* pp. 3–242, and *De Tradendis Disciplinis,* pp. 243–437; it is this latter section which Watson translated in his *Vives: On Education.*

[119] This is Watson's opinion: Watson, *Luis Vives: El Gran Valencian,* p. 72.

language of the *devotio moderna,* the *Imitation* proclaims
a religious dependency on God and a somewhat individ-
ualistic asceticism required of Man the Sinner. Philosophical persuasions rest lightly there and properly so, since
the spiritual classic was designed as a manual of devotion
and direction in the ascetical life.

The *Introductio* accepts implicitly the same call to
righteousness, the same practice of virtue, the same spirit
of prayer. However, it is more than a statement of belief
in God; it clearly makes an act of faith in man. To
principles of theology and classical philosophy, it adds
a summary of psychology, ethics, hygiene, and courtesy.
In a word, the *Introductio* posits in seminal form the
beginnings of a valid Christian anthropology.

THE CHANGING ROLE OF RATIO

The chronology of humanism lends itself to dispute. Is it
to be dated in the fourteenth and fifteenth centuries, as
Burkhardt suggests,[120] instituting a conclusive break with
the Middle Ages in its rejection of the traditional philosophy and theology of a unified Europe? Or did it
begin in Haskins' twelfth-century world,[121] and reach a
culmination in the fifteenth? Is humanism to be considered a movement at all; or in terms of its definition
by the very Renaissance personnel, is it primarily a matter of curricula and educational directions influential
only in the centuries beyond its own time?[122]

By the third quarter of the sixteenth century, the

[120] Jacob Burkhardt, *The Civilization of the Renaissance,* translated by S. G. C. Middlemore (Toronto, 1939).
[121] Charles Homer Haskins, *The Renaissance of the Twelfth
Century* (Cambridge, Mass., 1955).
[122] Paul Oskar Kristeller, *The Classics and Renaissance Thought*
(Cambridge, Mass., 1955).

Renaissance in England, of no matter which definition, was a *fait accompli*.[123] Above all, Tudor humanism refracted into a multidimensional splendor. Over the Renaissance years the brightness of intellectuality, emphasis of *ratio,* changed from classical rationalism to an openly scientific empiricism, from a theory of universals to the immediacy of experimentation. Vives contains the promise of both extremes. He stands convinced of the possibility—indeed, the obligation—to integrate both elements within the totality of man's person. The perennial tension between faith and science, the sacred and the secular, is resolved for him by, and in, the human person whose unified being permits no such cleavages. Empirical evidence is necessary, yes—look to his analysis of naturestudy.[124] Yet all the evidence from sense is merely grist for the mind and soul.

Two mutations of the *ratio* concept evolved in the Tudor years. The first took the form of the ideal of "the gentleman." He was no longer the uncouth boor of a half-century before, but a man of courtesy who cared about his speech, his clothing, his manners, his reading, and his destiny on the land or in the government. If the sons of gentry were sent to the schools of the countryside, they were polished off in the universities and the Inns. Their marriages were bargained with an eye to "rational" refinement. In this form of Renaissance *ratio,* the Tudor school played its role well. Its curriculum and academic atmosphere anticipated the gentleman's judgment and action. Regrettably, in time this peculiar

[123] Douglas Bush, *The Renaissance and English Humanism* (Toronto, 1939), pp. 74, 78, 80.
[124] Watson, *Vives: On Education,* pp. 163–171; also Foster Watson, *The Beginnings of the Teaching of Modern Subjects in England* (London, 1909), p. 157, and many other references to geography, mathematics, cosmography, etc.

rationalism turned to mere formalism, and hypocrisy had
its own renaissance.

In a second variant, the dominance of reason brought
with it an undue regard for its power rather than its
intrinsic worth. Education became an instrument of progress, a kind of social investment. Once designated as a
means to the knowledge, love, and efficacious service of
God through service to the world, education eventually
became an object of merely utilitarian purpose and
social elevation.[125] In this sense, the cherishing of reason
contributed within a curious complex of social, political,
and economic conditions to a growth of English nationalism, class delineations, and surface morality.

INROADS OF SKEPTICISM

What was happening in the sixteenth century was recognized by some thinkers even as the event occurred:
reason served to disbar reason.[126] In science, the insistence
on radical empiricism newly extolled the value of sense
evidence. In theology, the emphasis on faith loudly denied the inherent capacity of reason.[127] An over-riding

125 Still other references, added to Lawrence Stone, Joan Simon,
and Kenneth Charlton, cited earlier, are Fritz Caspari, *Humanism
and the Social Order in Tudor England* (Chicago, 1954; New York,
1968), and Paul N. Siegel, "English Humanism and the New Tudor
Aristocracy," in *Journal of the History of Ideas,* XIII (1952), 450–
468.

126 Hiram Haydn, *The Counter-Renaissance* (New York, 1950),
p. 83, quotes Richard Hooker, *Of the Laws,* Book III, chap. 8,
p. 4. Haydn sees humanists only as classicists who prepared the
way for a blatant Ciceronianism and meaningless verbalism. He
suggests that Vives, with his "philosophy of the particular," was
typical of the thinkers who laid the final blow to Christian humanism, a position which does not coincide with a reading of Vives'
writings. See also Paul Kristeller's review of Haydn's text in *Journal
of the History of Ideas,* XII (1951), 470–472.

127 For a survey of skepticism in its historical growth and de-

conviction of man's capacity to do anything, and the antithetical belief in man's total dependence on God, consorted to produce a skepticism in man's capacity to reason. In effect, the ambivalence of sixteenth-century man caught between rationalism and fideism never adequately resolved itself. The compromise—an intellectual religiosity and a theological scientism—remained into the seventeenth century. Christian piety did not perish, as the spiritual literature of the Puritans bore eloquent witness. Nevertheless, integration between piety and intellectuality had been irrevocably weakened in that tortured century.

Quite contrary to these later developments, Vives' fundamental realism, along with his Christian awareness of the origin and weakness of man, strongly rejected this threat of radical doubt. Yes, he had insisted on a kind of relativity in knowledge, as a tacit condemnation of the university men always so ready to defend their unfounded absolutes.[128] In the relation between God and man Vives pointed to the hiddenness of divine knowledge in itself, of future events, of the essence of the Godhead, or the specificities of God's supernatural works. Nevertheless, this is not skepticism but an honest appraisal of the human mind in the presence of omnipotence, an acceptance of evidence valid in terms of the whole of human nature. Once he had said, ". . . it is very seldom that we can affirm anything as absolutely true. It has not as yet been taken possession of. Much of

---

velopment within the Renaissance, as well as before and after, see Richard H. Popkin, *The History of Scepticism from Erasmus to Descartes* (Assen, 1960), especially chaps. 1 and 2, for this period.

[128] Haydn, *The Counter-Renaissance*, pp. 17–18. See Vives throughout the *Introduction to Wisdom*; also Watson, *Vives: On Education,* pp. 211, 166, 168.

truth has been left for further generations to discover."[129]
This is not skepticism, but rather a humanism which
accepts the limitations of created nature. Rejecting the
superficialities of quibbling academics, it rejoices in the
potentials of human existence. His view does not so
supernaturalize man that reality is negated; God's su-
pernal being is not so minimized that creaturehood is
granted undue powers. For Vives promptly recognizes
the loftiness of arcane knowledge wherein human equipment—even in the generations to come—will never penetrate mysteries which are divine in their essential being.
At the same time, he never doubts the capacity of that
richly endowed human nature to arrive at true knowledge
in a world of particulars.

THE GENESIS OF ORDER

Where the ancient Greeks and Romans had sculpted
their distinctive concept of order in Parthenons and
temples, English humanists executed theirs in society.
The "eternal chain of being" had already bound the
world and man into relation with each other, and each
to God. What the theorists newly devised was a political
relation between man and man. They did not create a
new structure of society, but rather shaped society to
their own design.[130]

Order and degree demanded authority and obedience.
From the first battlecry of Henry VII on the fields of
Botsworth to the last glowing words of Elizabeth's
"Golden Speech" to Parliament, the Tudors had com-
manded undeviating obedience, this to preserve a cru-
cially vital order in society. Ironically, while English

---

129 Watson, *Vives: On Education*, p. 9.
130 Caspari, *Humanism and the Social Order*, pp. 6–7.

law enjoined conformity as essential to the commonweal, the orderly alignment of societal arrangements was systematically annihilated. The regularity of a once harmonious social and political existence shattered at the break in ecclesiastical order.

If civic hierarchy had been broken, another must be built.[131] In Italy, Machiavelli had provided for the emergence of power politics; in England, it was a gentler rationalizing which made the King like to God. If God rules the heavens, He has appointed men to rule the earth. In the individual's life, an increasing reliance on the power of the human will substituted for the older unquestioning confidence in authority.[132] It is precisely in man's freedom and liberty that discipline should be introduced in order to preserve the essence of order.

In his *Introductio ad Sapientiam* Vives had placed universal order at the center of his philosophical and theological structure.

This is the order of Nature: that wisdom governs all things; that all creatures which we see obey men; and that in man, the body is obedient to the soul; and the will to the mind; and the mind to God. If anything deviates from this order, it is in error.

Man stands midway in the hierarchy. He has the power to control the world; he has the obligation to submit to God. His most difficult task devolves on the demand for compliance from his own wayward humanity. Without this harmony, the submission of the world is farcical and obedience to God is meaningless. For Vives, order in the world begins with order in, and through, the self.

Tudor schools varied in their standards, in their

---

131 As in law; see Haydn, *The Counter-Renaissance*, pp. 131–175 for the "repeal" of universal law; also Caspari, *Humanism and the Social Order*, p. 118.

132 Haydn, *The Counter-Renaissance*, p. 55.

equipment, and in their history of establishment or re-foundation. Accepting as many as 120 boys in a few instances, their charters more likely suggested numbers between twenty and forty.[133] The scholar's typical day lasted from six in the morning until five at night, tightly scheduled with declamations, disputations, double translations, compositions, and memorized recitations. In general, all students met simultaneously in the large lecture halls, then separated into their respective forms on banked benches. One master and one usher, usually assisted by older students, divided their instructional responsibilities throughout the day.

Scholars learned order through their social environment. If nothing more, their dress—carefully copied from adult styles—compelled a physical attitude of restraint and maturity.[134] In the discipline of the classroom the classical position maintained that the liberty of humanism would only follow upon the containment of disorder. Children would discover order in their school world through the chastisement of flogging, ordinary punishment in the schools. Humanists pleaded seriously against this practice. Elyot and Ascham, like other pedagogical reformers, insisted that scholarship was better served by the scholar who studied than by the master who flogged. Vives' hierarchy of penalties for the wrongdoer moved from love which "takes hold of him with its gentle hands," through reverence for the master, and only then to fear and threat of physical penalty.[135] Strictly

[133] Brown, *Elizabethan Schooldays*, p. 8. For specific descriptions see Nicholas Carlisle, *A Concise Description of the Endowed Grammar Schools in England and Wales* (2 vols.; London, 1818).

[134] Lu Emily Pearson, *Elizabethans at Home* (Stanford, Calif., 1957), p. 595; R. J. Mitchell and M. D. R. Leys, *A History of the English People* (New York, 1956), Plate XIV.

[135] Watson, *Vives: On Education*, p. 71.

speaking, punishment would be superfluous in the true student of wisdom, for he guides himself toward upright and desirable goals.

Like the teacher who prized eventual cooperation in a subdued pupil, the government valued the tranquility of an ever orderly populace. In the hands of three superb tacticians—the two Henrys and Elizabeth—domination by government injunction displayed brilliant strategy.[136] In the hands of over-riding Stuarts it collapsed into royal dictatorship under pious phrases like "divine right." In any age, a benevolent authoritarianism inclines to constructive growth, yes, but threatens personal subversion. Thus, Tudor political controls in education operated through Acts of the Privy Council, Royal Injunctions, and government-sponsored Canonical Visitations. The license to teach, the selection of grammar and catechetical texts, permitted readings, the right to publish without previous censorship, school construction—all these ordinary prerogatives of educators were denied free exercise by a government which treasured uniformity for religious and political reasons. In a sense, this development proved merely the logical extension of ecclesiastical control over medieval education. What made the situation unique, and eventually destructive, derived from the union of Elizabethan Church with Elizabethan State. Two fully primed mechanisms, so joined, become doubly effective in their results, both positive and negative.[137] Conceivably, a myopic account

[136] Background for the following development depends on a collection of texts too numerous to note. Typical titles include G. R. Elton, *Tudor Constitution* (Cambridge, Mass., 1960); Elton, *England under the Tudors;* David Harrison, *Tudor England* (London, 1953); J. D. Mackie, *The Earlier Tudors* (Oxford, 1952).

[137] Much has already been written on the control of the Tudor schools. See Foster Watson, *The Old Grammar Schools* (Cambridge,

of the differences between the Eton system and the St. Paul system might overlook the importance of the administrative nexus in which both procedural plans were developing.

PSYCHOLOGY, RATIONAL AND EXPERIMENTAL

With intent Vives' little "introductions" avoided scholastic disputation. He himself had regularly lashed out against mere wrangling in the philosophical centers. Here, by design, he meant to be persuasive through indirection; here his science takes practical directions. What is "mind" for Vives? The problem of translation from the Latin is compounded by the use of technical terms. The word *anima* generally means *soul*; however, both Vives and Morison used it properly as *mind* in specific contexts. Such liberty flourished legitimately in a sixteenth century which did not distinguish the field of philosophy from the field of psychology. Easy movement from one discipline to another characterized prescientific humanists. With his perceptive insight, however, Vives stands at once as classicist and innovator. No other humanist had systematically studied the elements of mental activity.[138] He introduced an empirical inductive method decades before Bacon or Descartes. As an early contributor to its scientific analysis, he validly merits the title of "Father of Modern Psychology."[139]

England, 1916), pp. 68–83; Watson, *English Schools to 1660*, pp. 10–79; A. Monroe Stowe, *English Grammar Schools in the Reign of Queen Elizabeth* (New York, 1908); Charlton, *Education in Renaissance England*, p. 94; Simon, *Education and Society in Tudor England*, pp. 136–148, 299–332.

138 William Harrison Woodward, *Studies in Education during the Age of the Renaissance, 1400–1600* (Cambridge, England, 1906; New York, 1968), p. 135.

139 Watson, "Father of Modern Psychology," p. 334. Colish, "The

To summarize his position briefly: mind, a dynamic part of the soul, uses reason, judgment, and intelligence, three facets of the same power. Thus ". . . strength of intelligence is given to the mind to weigh every single thing, to know what good is to be done, and what left undone." Such judgment does not exist in a vacuum; hence, it expresses itself and "is exercised and exhibited in many arts, both human and divine." It responds to experience of every type by which it is "sharpened and instructed." Because of its primary function of knowing "precisely the nature and value of each and every thing," it can teach the will what is of worth.

In the psychosomatic relationship Vives held to the supremacy of an ordered hierarchy in both body and soul. The body is to serve the mind, never permitted a precedence of authority. Mind is enervated by excessive food or sleep. Like a pampered horse throwing its rider, a delicately handled body may cause ultimate damage to the mind. Christian humanist that he is, he desires for man's mind and body an order based on the rationality of God and of man.

Nor did he develop the same refined distinction between mind and volition which later theologians and philosophers employed in the problem of free will. However, his support of the tradition of man's freedom and responsibility is implied in every exhortation he makes with his 592 "introductions." Further, it can be discerned in his analysis of wisdom, a virtue conferred on the judgment so that the will may choose sagely in all concerns, not merely that of morality.

Anything which compromises the superiority of the rational part of man must necessarily be considered in-

---

Mime of God," p. 18, does not agree with Watson's judgment in this matter of trail blazing.

ferior and subject for discipline. On the other hand, anything which serves the better performance of the mind must be fostered and appreciated. Standing as they do between soul and body (although with their inclination to earth), the emotions demand both reverence and control. For example, as a humanist opposed to war and cruelty, Vives dramatizes the horror and irrationality of anger, "the most atrocious of all the perturbations." In the best of clinical observations he notes that "it erodes the heart and afflicts the health," provokes unhappy social relations, and upsets the tranquility which brings restful sleep.

In an early work he had categorized emotions into four divisions:

1. Sorrow: emulation, swearing, spite, vexation, mourning, sadness, lamentation, care, doubt, troublesomeness, affliction, desperation.
2. Fear: sloth, shame, error, timorousness, amazement, disturbance, and anxiety.
3. Joy: exultation, delight, boasting.
4. Desires: wrath, fury, hatred, enmity, discord, need, and affection.[140]

Later he shaped a more elaborate scheme which resembles the approach-avoidance concept of conflict in modern psychological theory.

1. Motion toward good:
    a. Love: pleasure, favor, reverence, mercy
    b. Delight: joy
    c. Hope: desire

[140] Vives, *The City of God*, Book XIV, chap. 3, p. 500. Compare this with any modern general psychology text, such as Delos Wickens and Donald Meyer, *Psychology* (New York, 1961), pp. 226–264, or with James B. Watson's behavioral emotions of fear, rage, love, and grief.

2. Motion away from the evil:
    a. Offense
    b. Hate
    c. Grief
    d. Fear
    e. Longing
3. Motions against the evil:
    a. Against present evils:
        1. wrath
        2. envy
        3. resignation
    b. Against future evils:
        1. confidence
        2. audacity[141]

Such broad theories of affectivity underbrace the *De Anima* and the *De Disciplinis*. While not fully developed scientific psychological treatises, they nevertheless introduce the unadorned elements of psychosomatic relationships, of systematic classification, and of personality effects, all radically novel for his day and not inappropriate for the present.

The memory consists of three parts. In the first place, simple recall exists as a spontaneous power shared by men and animals alike. Second, reminiscence—the power to forage within the storehouse of remembered things—can move from one image to another. Two phases characterize this aptitude: consideration, or a rummaging in the mind; and recall, or the actual discovery of the matter sought. Finally, recollection occurs, the result of a reworking of the memory data again and again when the desired material cannot first be found. He early recognized the procedures and results of psychological

141 Baxter, "The Educational Thought of Juan Luis Vives," p. 185. Compare this with Kurt Lewin's theory as described in Wickens and Meyer, *Psychology,* pp. 202–214; or Kurt Lewin, *A Dynamic Theory of Personality* (New York, 1935), pp. 66–113.

conditioning, significantly studying it as a phenomenon of memory rather than as pure physiological behavior.[142]

In relevant addenda to the history of the *Introductio,* it should be noted that English boys had to learn Vives' translated sayings by heart, translate them into acceptable Latin, and then recite their compositions from memory. Actually, the Spanish humanist had planned his dialogues with that mnemonic function in mind, the *Introductio* to be rather a manual for stimulating reflection and moral action. Instead, English schoolmasters converted it into a grammatical device whose moral philosophy hopefully was transmitted in the memorizing process, a psychological position with which Vives may not have enthusiastically agreed.

MORAL PHILOSOPHY, THE KEY FACTOR

Vives' moral philosophy stems exclusively from his Christian humanism. Based on a solidly rational understanding and acceptance of the nature of man, it bespeaks man's potential for natural perfection and supernatural holiness. His propositions do not share the polemic of either Wittenberg or Trent. His norms for the upright moral life reflected Protestant as well as Catholic standards of right living. Hence, Roman and Reformed students alike studied and accepted his ethical principles.

Underlying Vives' assumptions of worthy conduct is the Augustinian notion of "seeds" of virtue planted within human nature, an inborn inclination to justice.[143]

[142] Baxter, "The Educational Thought of Juan Luis Vives," pp. 141, 152. Baxter's comment touches on the modern psychological "discoverers" of conditioning, noting that it is astounding to find such perceptions almost four hundred years before Watson and Pavlov.

[143] Baxter, "The Educational Thought of Juan Luis Vives," pp. 69–71.

Such readiness for virtue requires only nourishment and care to bring its operation to effective performance. The nature of children is not vitiated, but rather inclines to good, needing only responsible assistance and continuing creative guidance in its growing consciousness.[144] Without careful tutelage such "seeds" may disintegrate and degenerate, whether through idleness of the self or by deliberate mismanagement and miseducation by others. Far from falling into the "Socratic error"—knowing good is sufficient guarantee for doing good—he recognizes the fact of sin and wrongdoing, but only as the perversion of this natural bent toward virtue.

Such a balanced examination of the human estate suggests important pedagogical outcomes. In the matter of intellectual training and discipline he leans neither to the dour Calvinistic tenet of a depraved nature controllable only through brute discipline, nor to the undifferentiated Rousseauian dogma of a nature totally and irrevocably good in itself. Rather, he highlights the importance of the teacher, the *educ*-ator, the one who *educit*, leads out, draws out, builds upon the child's raw potential. He postulates a psychology of creativity and learning which admits in children inborn powers otherwise denied, or at least unexplored.

The readiness of the mind to recognize the good as naturally and as adequately as it comprehends the true, suggests the power of "conscience" in the technical sense—that is, reason making a judgment in the moral field. As with any structural function, when the natural quality of the mind to comprehend operates properly, satisfaction and delight follow. He would call on Cicero

144 Watson, *Vives and the Renaissance Education of Women*, p. 128; Vives, *The City of God*, Book XVI, chap. 26, p. 603; Book XIX, chap. 2, p. 755; Book XIX, chap. 4, p. 756; and Watson, *Vives: On Education*, p. 21.

and Horace to affirm the intense bliss of a pure conscience, the exquisite torture of a guilty one.[145]

Generally, then, his whole notion of morality directs
the person toward God through the trained judgment
and the aroused will. The individual arrives at his goal
through the guidance of mature preceptors. Hence, he
would oppose independent exploration by the untrained,
immature mind; he would censor heretical authors for
young students; he would especially restrict the freedom
of girls and young women with all the rigor of the
Spanish mores of his times; in brief, he accurately defined the genus of human knowledge, but firmly believed in the careful shaping of its species.

Although the *Introductio ad Sapientiam* reaches beyond mere moral philosophy (as witness its theological
and psychological wealth), at least 108 of the "introductions," or roughly 20 per cent of the work, specifically
concerns ethical matters. A distribution of topics shows
that Vives touched on actions of the person in relation
to the self, to others, and to God. In turn, these can be
fairly easily divided into the natural and the supernatural, that is, into acts which are attainable either through
a natural and ethical capacity or through the assistance
of what the theologians call "grace." Perhaps in no
other instance is the notion of Christian humanism
clearer than in these lines. Right living, defined according to ancient philosophers, has been baptized in the
doctrine of Christ. Religion and morality have been
integrated in practice, description, and application. This
is the marriage of grace and nature, of philosophy and
theology, of natural good and supernatural holiness.

Hence, the reader of the *Introductio* surveys the

[145] Vives, *The City of God,* Book XI, chap. 12, p. 419; Book XIX,
chap. 11, p. 766.

entire gamut of virtue and vice, both in general and in particular. Pride and humility, avarice and poverty, evil self-love and honest self-esteem are analyzed. Caution against undue and excessive indulgence of the body is frank and undisguised. He praises truth-telling, suggests fraternal correction, and frowns on flattery. He forbids grudges and oaths. He proposes an entire code for keeping secrets and requires control of the tongue in terms of charitable obligations. High-principled example to others he commends, while curiosity about the personal lives and thoughts of others he censures. One's life is to be a matter of honest deeds, not empty words. He denounces war and commends peace, not with the detail of his other works but with no less earnestness.

He eulogizes friendship in cadenced lines of personal faith. He suggests a fundamental respect for one's friends if for no other reason than not to lose them. Friends do not merely "happen"; they are chosen deliberately, rationally, and wisely. Such elected comrades will not only be personally enhanced because of their choice of each other, but also will be assured of an enduring love. Thus, written five years before Erasmus' unfeeling rejection, Vives' words significantly reflect his life-long constancy in friendship.

Still another element of natural goodness interweaves the *Introductio*, the significant section on manners and courtesy. Early sixteenth-century man was boorish, unmannerly, discourteous, unkempt, and unbelievably vulgar in his bodily actions. From royalty to commoner, the entire population practiced excesses of personal disorder and social irreverence which astound, if not disgust, the latter-day reader. Accordingly, the fundamentals of delicate behavior which Vives counseled needed constant elaboration.

In summary, the moral philosophy of the text brings
a self-insight to the learner which profits both philosophical and theological ends. With it he will become at
once a better child of God, a more honest citizen, a
truer friend, a more excellent scholar, a more complete
person. Habit and prayer will build toward holiness,
but knowledge of the good must precede. The science of
ethical living, moral philosophy itself, confers the hope
of virtue on the man who seeks for wisdom.

THEOLOGICAL OVERTONES

Five years before the *Introductio* appeared, Martin
Luther had thundered an ultimatum; soon he would
fashion a theology to cleave all Christendom. However,
when Vives was writing in 1524, Europe still pledged its
loyalty to Roman Catholic doctrine even while quarrel-
ing with its authority and its administration. In the
early unsophisticated perception of the conflict, no one
doubted his own membership in the Church. Vives simply
does not consider sects. He wrote for boys who would
know what he meant when speaking of the "Christian
religion." Everything he wrote in the *Introductio* was
penned within that context.

For this reason he makes no references to the organiza-
tion and administration of ecclesiastical matters, to
papal authority or sacramental theology, to credal doc-
trines and liturgical practices. All this he assumed.
When the ecclesial communities which had severed from
the Roman church took a visible structure, what Vives
had written in one context fitted almost without flaw
into the new setting of a religion formally and materially
different from what he personally held. Thus, members
of a variety of congregations each perceived a different

theological stress, even as they read at the same sources. To this must be added the fact that some theological dogmas are shared by all who call themselves Christians, regardless of their divergencies. In such a setting Vives' theology did not detract from his popularity, even when differences in dogmas ordinarily paired with bitter enmity.

To all Christians, man is a created being who is wonderfully sustained in existence by an omnipotent God. We are all made of the same elements by that Creator, so that if one man were to contemn another for low birth, it would be a tacit reprehension of God "Who is the author of every man's nativity." Like the father of a household, He governs His world with peace and power, with equity and wisdom (even though His ways are unknown to us). Such a consideration forces Vives to a reverence and honor for God which is total and irrevocable.

Even though he stands in awe of the Godhead, he moves with joy and lightheartedness, for he has received the assurance of friendship with this provident Creator through obedience to His will. Christ is the Way "on which we might steadfastly chart our journey God-ward"; He is the means by which we have come to know God; He is the model Whose life is the perfect pattern for us to follow. Perhaps with memories of the ships loading at his doorstep on Wool Market Street in the Bruges Spanish Quarter, Vives warns against excess riches and possessions as a dangerous overloading for a man on life's journey.

Once man's origin and destiny have been admitted, the means to holiness touch on the immediate and the practical. The practice of charity receives extensive review, with eighty-nine "introductions" ranging over the loves of self, of man, and of God. Such charity soars to a culminating consideration of the Crucified Christ in His work of redemption. The humanist in Vives focuses on the practice of virtue in terms of the classical notion of *pietas* wherein personal godliness and social righteousness become synonymous. Man's whole perfection grows as much with his knowledge as with his action. All learning is of service to piety but is not equivalent to it. In his view, learning does not guarantee piety, although knowledge leads to goodness.

PEDAGOGY AND PRACTICALITY

For Vives, the ends of education both as a science and as an art reflected his definition of man. Though sin-tainted, the creature's rich potential commands a radical fulfillment in life: an obligation of service to others, an enhancement of the self because of his own excellence, and a worship of God as his first beginning and last end. His belief in an eternal life did not confuse his objectives. In his defined sense, the "whole man" of this world metamorphoses into the saint of the next.

Men like Thomas Elyot, responding to the spirit of Florentine activism, proposed the formation of loyal citizens and informed "governours" as an ultimate objective in education; training and curriculum thrust toward this over-riding goal. Vives, however, would judge such an educational aim as "proximate"; as such, it would not be less important, nor would studies and procedures differ. He would deny the interpretations which presume that proximate ends are not crucial to the concern of eternity, that in some way they can be separated from "ultimate ends." He would resist the suggestion that ultimate ends are sufficiently expressed in themselves that they can serve as goals to action without amplification in the practical order.

Far from encyclopedic in expression or number, still his pedagogical objectives apply universally in a variety of times and circumstances. The chief end of education is knowledge *and* virtue, a well-honed judgment coinciding with disciplined volition. When practical wisdom presides over the mental functions, the order and relation so introduced evokes at once an art and a science of learning.

In his psychological study Vives had specified seven degrees of intellectual awareness:

1. Perception, experienced through the senses
2. Imagination, for things absent
3. Consideration, for things known and retained
4. Reason, for extracting the hidden from the obvious, and the general from the particular
5. Intelligence, by which we come to know the essence of things
6. Contemplation, for the joyful rest of the mind in truth and beauty
7. Wisdom, for the knowledge of God[146]

In the student each of these grades of knowledge involves the use of several faculties. The objective of practical wisdom lies in a coordination of relationships among and within these various powers.

Rather than attempt an inclusive summary, Vives cites illustrations of the objectives in operation. Thus, the transmission of learning to others he sees as one generation's gift to the next, for the purpose of a continuing growth in wisdom.[147] The lifelong character of learning

[146] Baxter, "The Educational Thought of Juan Luis Vives," p. 25, paraphrasing *De Anima*, from Manjansius, ed., *Vives Omnia Opera*, III, 378 ff.
[147] Or, education is to kindle another's light from one's own; see Watson, *Vives: On Education*, p. 288.

confirms the never-ending function of wisdom. The practice of excellence whether in personal life or in studies is subsumed under this function of value and hierarchy. Proximate or remote, in theory or practice, education's only objective touches on the perfection of the whole man in terms of both a human and a divine vocation, as the excellent surgeon filled with holiness, the brilliant lawyer living in sanctity, the illustrious scholar possessed by grace.

VIVES' "CHRISTIAN WOMEN"

The Renaissance female had already aroused a century of discussion,[148] most of which suggested subservience, or at least neutrality, in the superior world of men. Thomas More broke from the pattern when he schooled his daughters in the highest academic skills. Vives' philosophy and psychology of a woman's education went on to answer the perennial questions: What is the place of woman in the world? How shall she be prepared for it? Men like Ascham and Elyot were to echo his answers.[149]

Spanish gentleman that he was, Vives' personal associations with women bore a mark of constraint unacceptable to modern custom. Yet, he could be loving, happy, unembarrassed, and gallant, too, as his letters and essays demonstrate. The memory of a sober, disciplined, yet affectionate childhood pervaded his recollections when he wrote of his mother, Blanche March. Her

---

[148] See Ruth Kelso, *Doctrine for the Lady of the Renaissance* (Urbana, Ill., 1956), for a collection of original sources and excellent commentary

[149] Thomas Elyot, *The Defence of Good Women* (STC 7658, London, 1545), of which sections are quoted in Watson, *Vives and the Renaissance Education of Women*, pp. 211–239; and Roger Ascham, *The Scholemaster*, Edward Arber, ed. (Birmingham, 1870).

son placed her name on a list of ancient saints and "those . . . more fresher" with the daring of devotedness.[150] In this inventory Vives entered the name of Clara Cervent whom, as early friend in Bruges, nurse in his illnesses, and later loving mother-in-law, he came to honor in his adult years. Margaret Valdaura elicited not only understandably effusive praise from her fiancé, but the approval and respect of friends such as Thomas More and Francis Craneveldt.[151] In her maidenhood, in her role as wife and widow, she wholly mirrored Vives' ideal "Christian woman." She brought to her humanist husband care for his health, support in discouragement and depression, and tranquility for his studies, as he was to write.[152] When the Plague broke out in Bruges in 1529, both she and Vives fled to the south to avoid its deadly infection. Yet at the earliest word of its abatement, she returned to the city, probably to continue her work as nurse to the patients in the Spanish Quarter. Whatever her quiet existence touched, it left only the memory of a generally acknowledged *rara pudicitia,* rare virtue.[153]

The bittersweet days of England had left him long thoughts of still other Renaissance ladies. He bore an honest admiration for Margaret Roper's learning. Less than a year after he had met the More family, Vives celebrated not only Margaret but also Cecilia and Eliza-

150 Watson, *Vives and the Renaissance Education of Women,* p. 208, quoting from *De Offici Maritii.*

151 De Vocht, *Literae Virorum Eruditorum,* Ep. 102, lines 7–16; Ep. 115, lines 15–25; Ep. 106, lines 6–12; Ep. 112, lines 9–16.

152 In *De Offici Maritii,* as in Manjansius, ed., *Vives Omnia Opera,* VII, 196, 198, 220.

153 Manjansius, ed., *Vives Omnia Opera,* I, preface and pp. 65–75 of Manjansius' *Vita.* See also Bonilla, *Luis Vives y la Filosofía,* p. 249; Watson, *Relaciones de Juan Luis Vives,* pp. 223–227; and Watson, *Vives: On Education,* p. lxxxii.

beth, and Margaret Giggs, in the pages of his essay on
the education of women. Mary Tudor was about twelve
years of age when the royal litigation between her parents began. Not young enough to miss the meaning of
the event, she was not old enough to be emotionally
independent of its tragedy. A wide range of causes undoubtedly shaped her into the dour Queen of the
fifties; some say that Vives' tutorials may well have been
among them. Yet his pithy adages, her own *Satellitiae*,[154]
deny this conclusion. Those maxims of gentleness and
love would hardly have lit the flames for Protestant
martyrs at Smithfield nor coined the unhappy epithet of
"Bloody Mary."

Catherine of Aragon lived and died with a valor and
bravado worthy of Ferdinand and Isabella. For a period of at least ten years she and her brilliant country-
man had shared an affectionate tenderness and deep
regard for each other. At their last meeting the Queen's
Spanish stubbornness and heroism clashed head on with
Vives' chivalry and cynical insight. He never saw her
again after that November meeting in 1528, never wrote
to her directly, although he continued to praise her
eloquently in print.[155] Today one last poignant memento
remains of their affection, the copy of the *De Institutione Foeminae Christianae* preserved in the Bodleian
Library. Probably Vives' presentation issue for Catherine in the halcyon days of 1524, its binding is adorned
with intricate designs, its printing rich on pages of vel-

---

[154] See selections in Watson, *Vives and the Renaissance Education
of Women*, pp. 151–158. What little is known about Mary in that
depressing period, 1527–1535, is summarized in Madden, *Privy
Purse Expenses of the Princess Mary*, pp. liii–lxvi, or H. M. F.
Prescott, *Mary Tudor* (London, 1958), chaps. 2 and 3.

[155] As quoted in Watson, *Vives: On Education*, p. lxxxi.

lum,[156] its lines redolent of Vives' knightly deference for one of his most admired "Christian women."

DISTINCTIONS IN WISDOM

Severed from the frame of philosophical reference to which the humanists were born, modern interpreters of Renaissance "wisdom" sometimes cloud the definitions of intellectualism and moralism,[157] its related facets. An implication occasionally persists that wisdom and prudence function as either/or concepts. Either they are intellectual or they are moral; either they lead to action or they lead to contemplation; either they are concerned with the sacred or they deal with the secular. Such judgments require careful delineation, if only to avoid analyses of a wisdom and prudence which are neither what they are in themselves nor what they were to the humanists.

In his *Introductio* Vives directly or indirectly refers to five forms of wisdom: first, the Person of Wisdom, the Son of God and Second Person of the Blessed Trinity; second, the intellectual virtue of wisdom infused into the soul at Baptism; third, the Gift of Wisdom, associated with the Sacrament of Confirmation; fourth, the natural virtue of wisdom residing in man's intelligence and granting him sagacity of judgment; and fifth, the virtue of practical wisdom, a skill in using all things according to their proper function, arising from judgment and experience. He has thus artfully joined a regenerated

[156] Gustave Ungerer, *Anglo-Spanish Relations in Tudor Literature* (Berne, 1956), p. 11.

[157] Others refer in passing to the concept, but a detailed survey was made by Eugene F. Rice, *The Renaissance Idea of Wisdom* (Cambridge, Mass., 1958).

Aristotelianism with a Catholic theology of nature and grace.

Additionally, the Spanish humanist distinguishes between prudence and wisdom. In the first place, prudence is about human affairs, whereas wisdom (whether natural or supernatural) is about highest causes. Prudence serves wisdom; it prepares for wisdom. Wisdom considers the very object of happiness. It contemplates God the Father, in the case of supernatural wisdom; or God the Intelligible, in the case of natural wisdom. Prudence, instead, considers the means of acquiring happiness, the means of coming to that restful scrutiny of God. Or again, if a consideration of the object of our happiness could ensure its possession purely through contemplation, then wisdom would be perfect. However, in this life, knowing wisdom is not identical with being wise. Still, a small participation in that wisdom is possible to the natural (and supernaturalized) intellect of man. Hence, wisdom is nearer to happiness than is prudence, which looks to the means and not to the end. By implication, the sum of Vives' "introductions" propounds such a happiness, the end toward which the reader is directed.

He further distinguishes within the virtue of prudence its elements of the rational and the ethical. In a sense, it straddles the intellectual and moral virtues. He assumes a central position between the traditional conservative concept of wisdom and prudence, and the moralistic empirical notion which was to be developed in the following century. The weighting of wisdom with preponderantly moral demands may indeed produce an ethical virtue—but with it, a change in essence. Post-Renaissance wisdom is not merely prudential; it is no longer wisdom.

The importance of wisdom to man lies in its effect on his life. To illustrate its pervasive character, it is possible to spin out categorical opposites, each with its incipient tensions, each so much a part of the ordinary man's existence.

Sacred	Secular
Other world	This world
Intellectual	Moral
Speculative	Practical
Personal good	Public good
Contemplation	Action
Individual	Society
Deduction	Induction
Mysticism	Asceticism
Adoration	Moral action
Ends	Means
Divine	Human
Church	Scripture
Future	Present
Soul	Body
Internalized self	Externalized self
Authority	Personal judgment
Sophia	Scientia
Liberal arts	Practical arts

Vives, the Christian humanist, stands midway between each, embodying in his position aspects from both polarities. He optimistically reasserts his belief in the restored integrity of man and the allness of God met in Christ. He understands man as a creature ordained to existence in a societal life; but man "in the world" must choose and perform acts which will bring him to a destiny of transcendental joy.

This wisdom urges both an intellectual and moral (therefore total) dedication of man to, and in, his own society which is only part of a larger divine life in God. This wisdom becomes possible only when the totality of man's person is acknowledged—his origin and destiny; his physical, psychological, and spiritual parts; his world and its furniture. With humble respect for the reader, yet pridefully aware of his honorable task, Juan Luis Vives penned the *Introductio ad Sapientiam* because he himself had already recognized, experienced, and with joy committed himself to wisdom and its dispersion.

Preface to the English Edition

1540

Preface to the English Edition
1540

By RICHARD MORISON

To the right worshipful master Gregory Cromwell, son of the right honorable Lord Cromwell, Lord Privy Seal: Richard Morison wishes much wealth, with continued increase of virtue.

Whoever describes adequately the duties which belong to an honest heart will also be acquainted with those three ladies who wonderfully maintain the joyful society of man's life, three who among the Greeks are called Charities; among the Latins, Graces. As one such I can only see infinite causes, most gentle Master Cromwell, why I ought with all force of body, all strength of mind, all alacrity and cheerful promptness of courage, study to show my gratitude, study to make you bear with one who desires (and yet who will never succeed) to be free of your debt.

The first of these three damsels is Bountiful Beneficence, a lady of lovely countenance and noble inner life, one who always longs, yet has what she longs for; always with child, and yet delivered; always profitting, and yet striving to profit; always helping, and yet desirous to help more. The Greeks sometimes name her Eurydomene, which signifies a large and plentiful giver; sometimes, Aglaia, which very word sounds among us of gladness. Even by her name she teaches that duty requires well-doing to be performed cheerfully.

The second lady is Thankfulness of Mind, never forgetting benefits received. Her name is Thalia, which signifies freshness or greenness because duty and honesty demand that all pleasures, all blessings received, always be fresh in memory, always be green, never withering, never fading, at all times flourishing.

The third lady is Euphrosyne, much like her sister Aglaia, a damsel full of solace and full of delight, continually devising by what means she may contrive pleasure for pleasure, and recompense kindness with kindness.

Authors of great name and wisdom envision these three to proceed hand in hand: the first always looks forward, not once casting her eye back, never regretting benefits given and past. The second and third perpetually behold the first with amiable countenance, with faithful eye of remembrance, and full intent of recompense, as far as power—fortified with sincere desire—within them lies. Under such clouds, sage and grave writers are wont darkly to insinuate things of great weight, things very necessary for the quiet and honest leading of man's life, things worthy to be embraced by all men, worthy to be enflamed and branded in all men's hearts. They perceive that moral precepts, pleasantly proposed in the elegant colors of witty fantasies, creep faster into our hearts, and tarry there with much more delight and profit, than they would if plainly spoken.

Therefore, as you now can see what these three ladies signify, you must also of necessity see how I am bound to owe you my heart and my service with all that they both may do for you. My Lord your father, being so greatly enamored with that lovely lady Eurydomene, how can

I attend upon the other two damsels before life leave me? Being environed with so many and ample of his benefits, how I wish that Thalia and Euphrosyne both report me to lack power but not good will (as I trust that both shall have good cause so to do). Certainly, if I had seen where either my little wit or poor heart might better have served his Lordship than this—opening to you, his dear and entirely beloved son, such precepts of virtue as may make you most like your noble father—there are no pains which could have kept me from doing it. Be assured, Master Cromwell, that if labor and heart may pay the tribute that love owes, you shall never need to arrest me.

This book was gathered by Ludovicus Vives, a man greatly conversant in all good authors, and highly esteemed for all kinds of learning. The book has undoubtedly much more lying in its heart than the title promises in the forehead. It is not only an introduction to wisdom; but if you go as it leads you, it introduces—and ushers in—wisdom to your life. It roots the love and desire of virtue in your heart, extirpating from it all manner of vice and all spot; it furnishes you with general precepts for every kind of life, for all ages, for all degrees and states of life. Such precepts, if you harbor them in your breast, will certainly be a great support, help, and comfort to your tender age. They shall bring about in your lifetime, with great pleasure and no pain at all, many things which otherwise experience—so often powdered with bitter remorse—would never be able to teach you.

It is as wise Socrates says, "Precepts of learning were invented in the beginning as a necessary support and succor for man's mind (which lacks knowledge and experience) just as a staff is given of necessity to bolster up a feeble body." Assuredly, I know of no one book untranslated which has half so many wholesome documents as this has; none that may so well lead you the right way to true honor; none where you may with more delight, or more hope for success, trace true nobility.

Follow your leaders; go on with your guide. You shall find all the steps and footholds whereby not only My Lord your father has climbed honorably to nobility, but all others who in fact are (or were at any time) noble. You shall find many things herein that will be like ornaments to men of wealth and esteem; many that will be like sure counselors to men assaulted with the surges of sour fortune; advisors bringing with them, besides right and honest consolation, a great deal of satisfying doctrine; finally, many that are like an unparalleled medicine for almost all diseases.

The book is now yours. I trust that as the jewels which it offers you are great, rare, and precious, you will see them laid up in a place proper for such riches. Lock them fast in the chest of your heart; give the key to Remembrance, that she may let them out and carry them home again at such times as you shall think convenient.

If you make these precepts yours, by use of their speaking as they teach you and working as they advise you, who shall have more cause to rejoice in this than yourself! Wherein can you more please My Lord your father's mind! What thing can more satisfy his desire! What greater comfort can come to His Lordship than to see you most like him in all circumstances! What greater honor for you than to tread in his steps! What higher pleasure to all those who love you both!

Your country knows what noble feats My Lord your father has wrought by Wisdom, lady-governor of all virtues. She knows how honesty should rejoice, and how truth and religion should hold up their hands to heaven to this purpose: that God has sent to so gracious, so prudent and wise a prince, a counselor so good, so wise and so faithful; to so noble a master, a minister so diligent; to such a highly courageous and virtuous king, a subject of such noble heart and inner life! I must leave off: I have entered into too long a matter for a short epistle.

Therefore, I can only desire with all my heart that it may please God long to preserve noble Henry VIII in all wealth and in all honor to reign over us, for the setting forth of God's honor, for the spreading abroad of His glory, for the magnifying of His name in all places. May He long preserve My Lord to the furtherance of the same! Finally, may you be heir of His Lordship's qualities and virtues, as well as of his honor and worldly dignity! Thus may Our Lord send you ever well to fare!

Introduction to Wisdom

By

JUAN LUIS VIVES

Introduction to Wisdom

ON WISDOM

1. True wisdom is to judge a thing correctly and to identify it for what it actually is. Wisdom neither covets the cheap as though it were precious, nor rejects the precious as though it were worthless; neither criticizes matters deserving of commendation, nor commends things deserving of censure.

2. From such foolishness springs every error of men's minds. For nothing is more destructive in human life than a corrupt judgment which renders to no object its proper estimate.

3. The opinions of unschooled people are pernicious because they generally judge things most unwisely.

4. Without a doubt they are great schoolmasters of error.

5. There is nothing we ought more to strive for than to lift the student of wisdom above the emotions of the common crowd.

6. First, all things should be suspect which a multitude approves with consensus, until one has examined them according to those norms which make of virtue a measure for testing all matters.

7. Then, let each man be familiarized, even from his childhood, with right judgments, and thus to mature with the years.

8. Let him seek the upright and flee the crooked, so that the custom of doing good shall almost become his nature. Thus, unless he is physically compelled, as if caught in combat, it will be impossible to drag him forcibly to commit evil.

9. The highest ends in life must be chosen early; habit will soon make this most pleasant.

10. The rest of our life depends on our rearing in childhood.

11. Therefore, in the sprint for wisdom, the first stride is that most celebrated axiom among the ancients, "Know Thyself."

THREE AREAS PERTAINING TO MAN

12. Man is constituted of body and soul. The body (like those of beasts) we have of the earth, and of such elements as those we see and touch.

13. The soul, a gift from Heaven, is like to angels, like to God Himself. Through this latter part man becomes godlike; as the greatest men of antiquity think, it alone is deserving to be judged human.

14. There are in the body qualities of beauty, health, integrity of members, strength, swiftness, delight—and their contraries, as deformity, sickness, lack of limbs, weakness, sloth, sorrow, and so on. All these can be either helps or hindrances to their possessor.

15. Within the soul are found learning and virtue, and their opposites, ignorance and vice.

16. Finally, external to man are riches, power, nobility, honor, dignity, glory, favor—with their contraries,

poverty, neediness, inferior lineage, low estate, dishonor, obscurity, and disdain.

ON THE NATURE AND VALUE OF THINGS

17. The queen and principal mistress of this world is
Virtue. All other things serve her as handmaids do
their mistress, if they wish to fulfill their ends.

18. I define virtue as a reverence toward God and man,
a right service of God and a love for man, all
joined to a willingness to do good.

19. All other things, if one evaluates them in terms of
this virtue, will never seem evil.

20. Those who first named these things good did not
feel about them as the common crowd does now.
These latter have so corrupted the true and essential meaning of things that many ideas have lost
their correct significance through radical change.

21. Thus we must understand where, when, and how
far things ought to be classified as good. For example, wealth is not precious stones, nor metals, nor
royal palaces, nor gorgeous implements of the household. Rather, it is wealth enough not to need such
things as are necessary for the support of man's life.

22. To be well spoken of in terms of virtue, this is
glory.

23. To be held in veneration by reason of virtue, this is
honor. Esteem overwhelmed by the amiability of
virtue, this is charm.

24. An honest man's opinion concerning another's high
virtue, this is dignity, that certain beauty of inward
virtue outwardly expressed before men's eyes.

25. To have many whom you may counsel satisfactorily and righteously, this is sovereignty.

26. To be known by some excellent act, or as being descended from virtuous stock, to conduct oneself worthily like one's parents, this is nobility.

27. A truly outstanding man is he who is fashioned in virtue by an inherently excellent nature.

28. Health is a disposition of the body which gives dominance to the mind.

29. Beauty is seen in those lineaments of the body which declare an inner splendor.

30. Strength and vigor sustain the exercise of virtue without weariness.

31. Pleasure—a pure, total, and continual delectation—arises only in those things which appertain to the mind.

32. If a man discuss and analyze these preceding matters according to the judgment of an emotional mob, he shall find them unmeet, deceptive, and quite harmful.

33. First, external things are related either to the body or to the soul; thus, riches refer to the maintenance of our life, honor to the support of our virtue.

34. The body itself is nothing else than a coverture or, better, a bondslave of the soul; therefore, nature, reason, and God Himself commands it to be subject, animal-like and transitory as it is, to that which is immortal and divine.

35. Furthermore, learning exists in the very mind itself for this purpose: that we may more easily know sin

and avoid it, and know virtue and attain to it, holding all other things to be superfluous. If learning does not accomplish this in him who has it, she leaves her whole duty undone.

36. What is life other than a wandering amid the many hazards which crop up on every side? With threats everywhere, its end, perpetually imminent, may occur without warning from the slightest of causes.

37. Hence, it is the highest folly to perform any evil or sinful act for coveting such an uncertain and frightsome life. Who is to say how long you are to live after your wrongdoing?

38. As it is in a journey, so is it in a man's life: the lighter and less overstuffed his baggage, the easier and pleasanter his travels.

39. Moreover, the nature of the human body is so ordained that it needs very few things. Thus, if a man would consider the matter closely, he would doubtless judge insane those who greedily and anxiously accumulate goods upon goods when so little suffices. Someone expressed the essence of riches astutely by thus analyzing them: "They are longlasting provisions for our brief life."

40. For riches, possessions, and apparel are useless in our journey. What is over and above the useful is of no help but to swamp us, like ships overladen with too great a freight.

41. Gold itself, if you do not use it, differs very little from clay, except that its custody disquiets you more, causing you to neglect other things of greater concern.

42. Money brings men to a kind of idolatry; for it, other things are undervalued, such as godly reverence and holiness.

43. I will omit the many deceits practiced and traps laid for riches, the many and sundry ways wealth comes to naught, and the many vices into which men are driven.

44. What else is clothing but the trappings of pride?

45. Necessity first invented the useful garment; luxury, the precious one; vanity, the elegant one. Great contention follows on competitiveness regarding apparel, which only teaches much that is superfluous and damnable. Thus, men seek to be honored for that which plainly declares their weakness.

46. Most riches—elaborate buildings, numerous and opulent household furnishings, precious stones, gold, silver, and every genus of ornaments—are designed and exhibited as a brag and a spectacle in other men's eyes, rather than for the use of those who possess them.

47. What else is nobility nowadays but a chance birth into this or that gentle blood, and a reputation induced by the foolishness of an unlearned people (whose opinion of nobility itself often is acquired by hypocrisy or other unjust measures)?

48. True and perfect nobility originates in virtue. Hence, it is a great madness for you to boast about your parents, if you are evil yourself and dishonor their noble acts with baseness.

49. Truly, we are all constituted of the same elements, and have one God, Father to us all.

50. So, to contemn low birth is tacitly to reprehend God Who is the Author of every man's nativity.

51. What else is power than an elegant encumbrance? If only man knew what troubles and cares lie therein, and what a sea of adversities! No one would be so ambitious for power that he would not fly from it as from an overwhelming misfortune. He would not, as the king said of old, stoop to take up a diadem if it lay before him on the ground.

52. How hateful it is to govern evil men!—how much more, if you are evil yourself!

53. Honor, if it does not originate from virtue, is depraved. Falsely given and wrongfully taken, it cannot bring delight to you if your conscience denies it to you. Even if honor do arise of virtue, it still is not similar to it. For doing good ought not to be called or taken for virtue when it is performed for desire of honor. Honor ought to follow upon well-doing, not be hoped for from it.

54. How can dignities be called dignities, or honors, when they accrue to most unworthy men and are acquired by deceit, ambition, avarice, and evil machinations? How much worse when they are conferred by the capricious will of a mob, that beast of many heads which does nothing according to reason and right judgment.

55. Glory is nothing other than, as is said, a vain puffing of the wind that fills fools' ears.

56. Honor and dignity are in him who confers them, not in him who receives them. Such glory adheres little, or not at all, in him who grants it. Its qualities are uncertain, wandering, iniquitous, and fleet-

ing, very like their parent, the mob, which in the
space of the same day, will both praise and commend, yet dispraise and damn the same man. We
see, therefore, that honor commonly flies fastest
from him who most seeks it, and goes to him who
is least concerned about it. The same is true of the
changeable mob.

57. Furthermore, what shall I say is born of these
things, sometimes foolish, sometimes mocking,
sometimes fleeting, partly evil? Often such a man
advances in honor because he plays well at ball; on
other occasions because he pours out his patrimony
on junkets, minstrels, and scoffers. But war, above
all—that is to say, unpunished robbery—you must
acknowledge as the most powerful advancer of men,
so foolish is the madness of the mob.

58. Let every man descend into himself, and there se-
cretly reflect upon this matter. There he shall discover how little attaches to him from fame, from reputation, from veneration, and from the honor bestowed by the people from which he would take glory.

59. What difference is there between the highest king
and the lowest slave when they are both asleep? Or
when they are in solitude?

60. Finally, everyone should be persuaded that nobility, honor, power, and dignities were born and are
a remnant of that twisted persuasion which Christ
erases from those who are truly His. The former
are sown like cockle by our mortal enemy, the devil,
among the good wheat of God.

61. What is beauty in the body?—only a well-colored
thin skin. If the inward parts could be seen, what

fetidness would be espied, even in the most beautiful! The fairest body is nothing else but a dunghill covered in white and rose.

62. What does clothing and comeliness in features or body avail if the mind be unclean, and if there is (as the Greek writer says) "a foul guest in a fair hostelry"?

63. For what purpose does strength of body serve when the greatest and most appropriate human values are not gained by strength of body but by gifts of the mind?

64. Our strength, be it ever so great, can in no way equal the strength of a bull or an elephant. It is reason, it is intelligence, it is virtue wherein we surpass them.

65. I need not emphasize that beauty, strength, agility, and additional gifts conferred on the body, wither away like little flowers and pass away through little mishaps. Infections, or a small fever alone, can strike down the mightiest man and take toll of the highest beauty.

66. Even if any mischance were not to come, yet every thing of necessity will deteriorate through age and yield to its ravages.

67. Therefore, no man can rightly count as his such externals which suddenly transfer to other men. No man can reckon things of the body to be his which flee away so swiftly.

68. What should I say about those things, which so many men astonishingly seek, and which become occasions of serious sins—such as insolence, arro-

gance, slothfulness, rage, envy, grudges, strife, wrangling, wars, floggings, murder, and manslaughter?

69. Sexual gratification is low and bestial, just as the body itself is. Often, irrational animals revel in it more intensely and longer than man.

70. Yet from these unlawful pleasures many diseases redound upon the body and cause irretrievable losses. Remorse inevitably affects the spirit; one's intellectual ability, weakened by pleasure, disintegrates; finally, hatred of all virtue settles in the soul.

71. Nor should such acts be practiced openly, for they do not reflect the nobleness of our mind. None are so depraved that they do not blush in the presence of witnesses. Such practices engender ignominy and shame; such who use them are rightly driven to seek darkness and secret corners.

72. Furthermore, their fleeting and brief pleasure can never be retained nor does it ever come unmixed or free of bitterness.

73. Lay aside the opinions of the common people. Do not consider the greatest evil to be poverty, low status, imprisonment, nakedness, ignominy, deformity of body, sickness, and mental debility. Instead, consider defects of mind as the greater evil, such as ineptness, incapacity for knowledge, dull stupidity, and stark madness.

74. Esteem as a great good their contraries, virtue and things related, namely, knowledge, quickness of wit, and soundness of mind.

75. If you possess anything else, whether gifts of fortune or gifts of body, they shall be beneficial to you if referred to virtue, detrimental if related to vice. If you have neither the one nor the other, do not seek them, even with the least expenditure of virtue. That would be like buying a little clay with a great sum of gold, or to change health for painful sickness. No greater advantage accrues to the soul than the increase of godliness; no greater gains to the body than to know how to use, and be content with, the present state of life, however simple it may be.

76. Deference received, even in excess, can be ultimately profitable. A good reputation, even though you have nothing to do about it (because it simply arrives), ought to be preserved in all its entirety. The regard for it prevents us often from wrongdoing and, additionally, is an example to stir other men to righteousness.

77. From this comes that wise precept of holy men: "You shall no evil do, nor anything which resembles it."

78. If we cannot attain to this high standing, well, we owe it to our consciences to be content and to avoid those human sentiments and judgments which, being so corrupt, count virtue to be vice. Then we must labor that God alone approve our inward and outward acts. His approval should be abundantly sufficient for us.

79. It is easy to turn the inconveniences of the body or the mischances of fortune to your profit, if you but suffer them patiently. The more promptly you adhere to the practice of virtue, the less will evils

afflict you and the more expeditiously will you advance in other matters.

80. Oftentimes, from suffering of body and loss of goods, great increases of virtue are engendered.

ON THE BODY

81. In this pilgrimage of life, we bear a soul enclosed within our body, a great treasure in a brittle vessel. Hence, it follows that we are not to repudiate or contemn the body.

82. Instead, we must so regulate it that it does not presume to be a master, or even a comrade, but rather a servant; nor should it presume support for its own sake, but rather for the soul's.

83. Whoever cherishes the body neglects the soul.

84. The more delicately the body is treated, the more stubbornly it wrestles against the mind, even casting it off, just as a horse pampered too much throws his rider.

85. The heavy burden of the body bears down on the mind. Stuffing and cherishing the body dulls the wit.

86. Food, sleep, all manner of exercise, and the whole governance of the body must be directed toward its health, not merely to its pleasure. Thus, the body may serve the mind more actively, neither waxing wanton in a wild body-worship, nor declining from lack of strength.

87. Nothing so much debilitates the quick vigor of the mind, and the strength and sinew of the body, as does voluptuousness. Body and mind thrive with

exercise and moderate labor; by idleness and wanton pleasures, their powers languish away.

88. Delicate or dangerous diets of meat and drink must be put aside. Cleanliness contributes both to physical health and to one's wit.

89. Wash your hands and face often with cold water, and dry them again with a clean linen towel.

90. Thoroughly clean those parts of the body from which the excrement of your inward parts emerges.

91. Often wash your head, ears, nostrils, eyes, armpits, and private parts.

92. Your feet ought to be kept warm and clean.

93. Keep the cold from the other parts of the body as well, but most especially from the nape of your neck.

94. Do not immediately eat on arising, and only a little before dinner.

95. Breakfast is meant for assuaging the gnawing stomach, or for refreshing the body, not for satiety.

96. Therefore, three or four morsels of bread should be sufficient, without any drink (or at least only a little); such is no less wholesome for the mind than for the body.

97. Accustom yourself at dinner and supper to eat of only one main dish—if your constitution will allow, one that is most simple and wholesome. Even if many courses are offered elsewhere, do not admit them to your table.

98. Diversity in foods can be harmful; diversity in seasonings, even more so.

99. A clean and pure regimen, coinciding with tem-

perate and chaste minds, is a great boon in a household for that, in itself, shows us how little we need. Let us commit no vulgar offense in hope of further indulgence, thereby the more to satisfy our tastes for excessively delicate, dainty, and out-of-the-ordinary dishes.

100. We shall do well, if we not only content ourselves with whatever we already have, but also share some of it with the needy.

101. Our Lord Himself gives us an example of this. When He had feasted the multitudes, He would not allow the leftover bread and fish to be thrown away.

102. Nature has taught us that necessary things are few and easily procured; folly has devised superfluous things which are without number and hard to acquire.

103. If you give necessities to Nature, she is delighted and strengthened, as with things thereby appropriate; but if you give her superfluities, she is weakened and afflicted as with things thereby alien.

104. As necessities do not suffice where folly craves, so superfluities only overwhelm rather than satisfy.

105. Your drink shall be either that natural liquor prepared by God for all living creatures in common—pure, clean water—or else the thinnest beer or well-diluted wine.

106. Nothing harms the body of young people more than hot food and drink, for it enflames their viscera, sets on fire their passions, and flings them headlong into rashness.

107. Do not imbibe after supper; but if thirst moves

you to do so, take something waterlike or cold—or a skimpy quantity of light liquor.

108. Between that potion and your going to bed, let there be at least half an hour.

109. Regarding the recreation of the mind, consider what little time has been given for that in man's life, and that it ought not to be squandered in games, in revels, in childishness, or in trifles.

110. How brief is the course of our life, even if every whit of it were used in adorning the mind!

111. We are not made by God for gaming or trifles, but rather sent to be occupied in sage matters, thus to attain moderation, modesty, temperance, religion, and all other kinds of virtue and honor.

112. You will not heal the sickness of your body with the diseases of the mind.

113. Exercises of the body should not be excessive, but used with reasonable regard for health. Here we should follow the advice of expert and skilled physicians.

114. Do this insofar as they do not transcend the limits of prudence in bidding us to do anything evil, immodest, impure, or scandalous. Additionally, in pastimes and refreshments of the mind, some remembrance of virtue should always be made.

115. Banish all arrogance, contentions, quarrelings, envy, and covetousness. What foolishness it is to torment your mind instead of studying to delight it! You are no wiser than those who put gall into honey which they actually prefer as sweet.

116. Sleep must be taken as a specific medicine, and as much only as is sufficient to refresh the body; for

excessive sleep brings the body to hurtful humors at once sluggish, lazy, and slow, and retards the swiftness of the mind.

117. The time which is spent in sleep is scarcely to be counted as part of life: "For life is a watch or a waking."

ON THE SOUL

118. There are two parts of the soul: one understands, remembers, and savors things as they are, using reason, judgment, and intelligence. This is properly called "Mind," the superior part, by which alone we are like God, far passing all other living creatures.

119. The other part which is called "Will"—"Animus" —is void of reason and, in conjunction with the body, is brutelike, fierce, cruel, more like a beast than a man. In this faculty dwell those emotions which are called either affections or passions: arrogance, envy, malice, anger, terror, depression, unsatisfied desire, and giddiness. This part is called inferior whereby we differ in no wise from beasts, and by which we flee most distantly from God Who is beyond all defect and passion.

120. This is the order of Nature: that wisdom governs all things; that all creatures, which we see, obey man; and that in man, the body is obedient to the soul; and the will, to the mind; and the mind, to God. If anything deviates from this order or perverts it, it is in error.

121. Therefore, it is sinful in man that his evil passions should rage and force their rule on the whole man,

contemning and disdaining the authority of the mind. Moreover, the mind abandons the law of God if it serves both body and soul.

ON LEARNING

122. Strength of intelligence is conferred on the mind to weigh every single thing, to know what good is to be done, and what is evil and to be left undone. Strength of will is of such great power that the soul must obey the will when the latter insists on it, nor will it yield one point of its sovereignty.

123. Intelligence is exercised and exhibited in many arts, both human and divine. It is much sharpened and instructed with great and admirable experiences in various matters. It thereby comprehends precisely each nature and every value, and so can teach man's will what good is to be followed and what evil to be eschewed.

124. Those crafts must be shunned which war against virtue, crafts which work by divinization, such as palmistry, pyromancy, necromancy, hydromancy, and astrology. In these are found the most deadly falsehoods, devised by the devil, our deceitful enemy.

125. For they touch upon and proclaim those things which God has reserved for Himself alone, that is to say, the knowledge of future and hidden matters.

126. We ought not to inquire into God's majesty or His arcane secrets (these being remote from our knowledge) with which He would not have men meddle.

127. He who searches out the greatness of God's majesty will be struck down and overwhelmed by this glory.

128. Therefore, Paul bids us to be only as wise as it becomes us, to be wise in moderation, saying that he saw hidden things of which no man can speak adequately. Also, Solomon, the discourser of the Hebrews, says, "You shall not inquire of things above your capacity, nor scrutinize things above your strength, but content yourself with what God has commanded you."

129. Think always on this, never being too curious about His many other works.

130. We must reject all arts invented by the devil with whom, as with enemies of God, we ought in no wise to have any dealings whatever.

131. It is not expedient for us to know the opinions of philosophers or heretics contrary to our Religion, lest that subtle and crafty spirit (the devil) inject into our hearts some scrupulous doubt which may excessively torment us and, perhaps, bring us to our destruction.

132. Authors who write wantonly ought not to be touched, lest any evil adhere in the mind like a contagion.

133. Evil communication often corrupts good conduct.

134. Learning is unsullied and fruitful only if directed to its proper end, virtue (which is to do good).

135. There is a divine knowledge handed down from God in which are hidden all the treasures of learning and wisdom. This is the true light of man's mind. All other learnings, compared with this, are the densest darkness, or like childish trifles.

136. Yet the latter are read for this intent: that our

Christian light may appear as if brighter from such a comparison.

137. Furthermore, they are read that we may use such knowledge as human testimonies for those who can less abide the Divine Scripture than sore eyes can abide the splendor of the sun.

138. When we perceive the practice of outstanding virtue in numerous classical pagans, we may well call to mind how much virtue becomes us Christians, disciples of our Master, God. It is He by Whom we know this Light of holiness, and are charged by no small obligation to live righteously.

139. Additionally, eloquence and its practice, added to a discipline of life, teach us about everything which we may ever need.

140. We fashion erudition by these three instruments: intelligence, memory, and diligence, which latter is also called study.

141. Intelligence is refined and made subtle with practice.

142. Memory is enlarged by exercise.

143. Delicate handling enervates them both; good health confirms them in strength; idleness and daily slackening put them to flight; exercise sets them to hand and keeps them in readiness.

144. Whether you read, or whether you listen, do it with attention. Do not let your mind wander, but constrain it to be present and to do that thing which is here, and no other.

145. If it swerves aside, call it back again, as it were, with a little word. Defer until another time all

considerations which may distract you from the studies at hand.

146. You should realize that you lose both time and labor if you are not attentive to what you read and hear.

147. Do not be embarrassed to learn things you do not know. Do not blush at what you must be taught, for great men have not been ashamed at that. Rather, blush if you are ignorant—and not willing to learn.

148. Do not boast of knowledge where you are ignorant; but rather search it out from those persons whom you believe to know the answers.

149. If you want to be taken for a learned man, conduct yourself like one. There is no shorter route to that end, just as you can by no other means more easily attain to esteem as a good man, than if you are so, in very deed.

150. Finally, whatever you wish to appear as, do that, in order to be that—otherwise, you wish in vain.

151. Time undermines the false and confirms the true.

152. Simulation does not endure.

153. Always follow your tutor, rather than run before him. Believe him: do not resist him.

154. Love him, and take him as your father, attributing whatever he says to be very true and certain.

155. Take care that you do not err again after having been corrected two or three times for your mistake. Instead, try to profit from the correction.

156. It behooves you to recall what has deceived you in the past, lest you be deluded by it again.

157. It is natural enough for man to err; but no one, unless he is a fool, would persevere in error.

158. Of all our senses we are most efficiently instructed by that of hearing.

159. Nothing is easier or more useful than to listen to many things.

160. Do not listen to frivolous, trifling, or ridiculing matters, but rather to those things which are earnest, wise, and weighty.

161. Both types of listening are absorbed with similar labor, although the advantage which rises from the one is far unlike the other.

162. Do not strain to make the wordiest responses; rather, be apt and brief.

163. Invite to your dinner and supper companions who are able both to make you merry with their pleasant and learned communication, and to have you rise wiser than when you sat down.

164. Do not admit to the honor of your table such as are scoffers, parasites, evil babblers, buffoons, drunkards, filthy and shameless hangers-on, gluttons, and such other types, ready either by their words or deeds to arouse lewd laughter. Those cannot refresh you at your repast. Rather, seek those who can with witty and learned conversation make you merry.

165. Not only forbid your mouth any defilement of speech, but also your ears which are, as a man should say, windows of the soul. Remember that saying which the Apostle cites, "Depraved communication often corrupts good habits."

166. Diligently listen to whoever is speaking, whether it be at the table or any place else.

167. In so doing, you shall learn of the wise to become better.

168. Of the foolish, you will learn to be more circumspect.

169. Pursue whatever the wise esteem.

170. Eschew what the foolish applaud.

171. If you perceive anything of wise men, such as is spoken fluently, seriously, learnedly, or urbanely, keep it in mind that you may use it yourself on occasion.

172. You should always have at hand a notebook in which you can jot down festive, elegant, or thoughtful things as you read or listen. Or perhaps you will note precise or rare words, useful for ordinary speech, which you may want to have in readiness for later use.

173. Do not strain merely to accumulate words, but rather to comprehend their meaning.

174. Retell in Latin whatever you have read or heard to your fellow-scholars. Speak in the vernacular to others unskilled in languages, endeavoring to repeat the matter with no less grace than when you first heard or read it. In doing this, you will have to exercise both your wit and your tongue.

175. Your style of composition—that tutor of eloquent speech—must frequently be exercised and stimulated.

176. Write, transcribe, annotate, and recopy often. Every other day, or at the least every third day, compose a letter to some person who will answer it.

However, show your copy to your master first for corrections, before you presume to send it. Make a note of whatever he brings up for correction so that you will not miss it again.

177. After eating, whether it be dinner or supper, relax from your studying. After dinner, sit down in some place where you may talk and listen to some pleasant conversation; or else, play at some game whereby you will not unduly exercise or disturb your body.

178. After supper, which I would suggest be light, walk with some merry company whose conversation is at the same time learned, and whose words and sentences you may imitate with good grace.

179. Between supper and retiring, avoid all kinds of liquor, for nothing is more pernicious to body or memory or wit. If thirst, nevertheless, obliges you to drink, then do not go to bed for at least half an hour.

180. Do not let your memory decay through idleness.

181. It rejoices above all things to be set to work and thereby to be augmented.

182. Assign it daily some worthy business.

183. The more often you commit matters to its custody, the more faithfully will it guard them; and contrarily, the less frequently, the more untrustworthy you shall find it.

184. When you have committed anything to its keeping, let it lie quiet for a while; then later, demand it back again, as a thing left for deposit only.

185. If you want to learn anything perfectly, read it most attentively four or five times at night—and

then retire. When you rise the next morning, demand from your memory what you delegated to it the night before.

186. Guard against overdrinking, indigestion, and catching cold, especially in the neck.

187. Too much wine not only poisons the nerves in man; it also kills the memory.

188. It is an excellent thing, a little before you go to rest each evening, to call to memory in solitude everything you have seen, read, heard, or done during the day.

189. If you have acted honestly, moderately, prudently, wisely, decorously, and deservingly, you should rejoice; acknowledge this as a gift of God, and resolve to continue in the same way.

190. On the other hand, if you have done anything base, immodest, outrageous, childish, foolish, or worthy of rebuke, recognize it as your own wickedness. Repent of it and resolve never to err again.

191. If you have heard or read anything elegant, learned, serious, or holy, keep it in mind.

192. If you have seen any commendable thing, imitate it, and shun the contrary.

193. Let no day pass that you do not read, or listen to, or write, something which will augment your knowledge, your judgment, or your virtue.

194. On going to bed, read or listen to something worth remembering. Let it be such that your dreaming of it may be both pleasant and delightful, that even in your night-visions, you may learn and become better.

195. No end is appointed for the study of wisdom in this

life since it ends only with life itself. It behooves man to meditate (as long as he lives) on these three things: how he may think well, how he may speak well, and how he may act well.

196. All arrogance must be excluded from his studies. Let him realize that even the most learned man alive is very little in comparison with the innumerable things of which he is ignorant. What men know is scanty, obscure, and uncertain. Our minds, being chained within the prison of this body, are oppressed with great ignorance and deepest darkness. We have only a blunted edge with which to break into the most significant aspects of things.

197. Furthermore, arrogance greatly encumbers the development of studies, for many might have come to wisdom if they had not considered themselves already arrived.

198. Contention, emulation, backbiting, and vain desires of glory are to be shunned; rather, the pursuit of studies assists us in escaping from the cruel dominion of those vices.

199. Nothing can be imagined more pleasant than the intellectual savoring of innumerable things, nothing more fruitful than the knowledge of virtue.

200. Studies are of such efficacy and strength that they temper prosperity, mitigate adversity, restrain the hasty and rash indiscretions of youth, delight and comfort the crooked and painful hesitations of old age. Whether at home or abroad, in public or private, in solitude or in frequentings, in business or in leisure, never absent but always present, they bring us aid and joy.

201. Learning is the truest food of the mind. Hence, it

is not proper for the body to be nourished and the mind to be kept hungry; for from the latter springs all that is pleasurable or delightful, secure or long-lasting. In studies, one branch gives birth to another, and each renews itself; nor do they ever leave us, or ever make us weary.

ON VIRTUE AND THE PASSIONS

202. Virtue, that excellent treasure surmounting all worldly riches, is not bestowed by man, nor is it achieved alone. It comes only from God.

203. Therefore, we must petition for it from Him with meek and humble heart.

204. The highest subject in the liberal arts and learning is that moral philosophy which brings a remedy for the deadly diseases of the soul.

205. A great deal of diligent labor is taken to cure the body; much more ought to be conferred on the soul since the latter's defects are more occult, more serious, more threatening and perilous.

206. These diseases are called—and not without cause —tempests, torments, tortures, scourges, bonds, and furies of the human soul. They bring with them great calamity and unbearable sorrow if they are permitted to reign and rage; and contrarily, incredible tranquility and beatitude, if they are conquered and controlled.

207. To that end this essay clarifies what the wise men of old have written about life and about custom with their penetrating talent.

208. This is the great reward and the true fruit which literati seek for their labors. They do not gar-

ner their learning proudly for the sake of admiration or ostentation. Rather, it is useful to all men in the first place, and then to the writer. Such learning is not like a box of precious ointments out of which salves are taken to delight other men, with the box itself remaining useless.

209. Christian religion strives for nothing so much as that its serenity may exhilarate human souls. The passions being at peace, it endeavors to make us resemble God and His angels in orderliness of mind as closely as possible.

210. Remedies for those above-mentioned diseases can be sought from external things and from ourselves, or from God and from the law and life of Christ.

211. The nature of things is such that they are all uncertain, unstable, momentary, and repulsive, the soul only excepted. It is the soul which is man's uniquely, and which is certainly his most precious part. All other things being so changeable, no man should call anything his own except his soul.

212. Whatever a man has, let him consider it not given permanently but, instead, lent for a season.

213. Hence, it is madness of judgment to commit any serious sin worthy of grievous punishment in exchange for a worldly trifle.

214. Let no man advance himself because the gifts of Fortune or of body have fallen to him, for these have only a brief future, being uncertain, inappropriate, and alien to us. Just as they are granted us, so they shall be required back again at the moment of death—and often, even in life.

215. Neither ought we be depressed if what was lent to us only or, as a man would say, given to our keep-

ing, should be asked back again; rather, it becomes
us to render thanks for having enjoyed its use for
so long.

216. It is intolerable ingratitude if, having had some
benefit for a while, you take injury if it does not
always continue; ingratitude, if you do not consider
what you have had and for how long, instead of
regretting what you have not had, or for how long
you have not had it.

217. Do not rejoice when what is withdrawn from your
enemies comes to you or your friends; for such is
the speed of Fortune, and such the uncertainty of
all things, that bitter tears often follow closely on
vain mirth.

218. Do not let your spirit be depresed although Fortune turn her face, for merry eventides do oftentimes follow adverse mornings.

219. Now, what is the state of man? What is life which
had such a vile and brittle origin that our existence
is endangered and beseiged on every side? Although
life seems sure for a little time, yet it will not long
endure. Therefore, what do we have that we should
be so ferociously possessive amid such weakness?

220. For this life is nothing but a pilgrimage in which
we reach out for eternal life, needing very few
things for the finishing of the trip.

221. What has this world worth longing for? Why are
we solicitous for things we see tossed and turned
about?

222. Why should we serve our never-satisfied appetite,
when the future is so uncertain and the present can
be content with so little?

223. He who longs only for those things of which he is sure is a free man. On the other hand, he is a bondsman who does the contrary.

224. Now, what else are we, when loaded with the gifts of Fortune, than foot-travelers encumbered and overburdened with too many packsaddles?

225. No man is so stupidly insane as not to prepare and fit himself more for the city where he proposes to dwell, than to make careful plans for the mere journey.

226. This life of ours is, of its nature, short and fugitive. The greatest part of it is completely lost in perturbation, in troubles, and imaginings. We do not live effectively, being shaken by our passions, and especially by the fear of death.

227. And whereas death, imminent as it is, may approach us by infinite ways, we ought not to fear its coming by this way and that. Since it must of necessity come, it cannot be escaped through any wrong means, nor mourned when it approaches.

228. Our life being oppressed with such innumerable and painful labors and miseries, why hold to it with such straining? Why set so much on it, seeing that we go to another life which is everlasting? Let us, rather, so order ourselves that we may go swiftly to that other eternal life which is filled with all that is good.

229. In conclusion, our errors oppress us, more often than reality itself; thus we judge them to be great evils, or great goods, when they are neither.

230. The nature, condition, and true value of things is such as I have proposed in the beginning. It is

apparent that there is nothing beautiful, nothing
of value, nothing which ought to be accounted
ours, except virtue.

231. Therefore, our inner judgment must discover this
inclination toward the love of our body, and the
desire of things here in this life, which is custom-
arily called our self-love.

232. Such self-love enervates the strength and virility of
our minds to such a degree that nothing can be so
minute but that it is easily able to penetrate
therein; nothing so slender or tenuous, but that it
may disturb them.

233. This disorder blinds the eyes of the mind. When
the passions have conquered the kingdom, we flatter them, we indulge them, we obey them as our
lords.

234. Hence, we hold with tooth and nail things not ours,
as though they were; and if they are withdrawn
from us, we bewail it and are afflicted with grief
as though we had a great loss.

235. We neglect our own goods as if they were not ours;
we reject what is of worth as though it were specifically poisonous; we embrace what is likely to damage, as being useful.

236. The troubles of other people seem the slightest to
us, and others think theirs greater than ours—and,
so, more intolerable. We are always attempting to
get what others have, as well as what we want
ourselves.

237. We are not content with ourselves; this world with
its laws does not satisfy us. We would like the nature of all things unchanged, such is the impatience
that grows of fanciful dreams.

238. What anguish can be compared with such troubles as these?—truly, the torments among the dead spirits are not greater.

239. The devils themselves have no other punishment than that they be vexed with pride, envy, hatred, and wrath.

240. Look at the countenance of those who are enmeshed by those passions, so many different kinds—anxious, breathless, murderous, and horrible. In like manner, their minds are racked within them.

241. Anger, which is the most atrocious of all perturbations, is most unseemly in a man.

242. Indeed, it changes his nature into that of a cruel beast.

243. Although every trouble obscures the judgment and keenness of the mind, anger overwhelms it with darkness so complete that it is unable to discern truth, or value, or comeliness.

244. It erodes the heart and afflicts the health.

245. It compels men to do things which bring only remorse.

246. What a deplorable change in the face! What sudden tempests arise there! What burning eyes, what gnashing of the teeth, what foaming of the mouth, what complete paleness, what stuttering of the tongue, what terrible shouts!

247. It is said, not without cause, that in their anger, some have seen themselves in a mirror and could not recognize themselves.

248. By his grim countenance, his sharp words, and cruel deeds, the angry man loses much of his authority and good will; his friends forsake him, passers-

by avoid him, and he is left all alone—for all men hate and abhor him.

249. Therefore, great wise men never guarded against, or cloaked over, a thing with greater diligence than they did anger and its effects. Thus, they wrestle against their own nature to bring it under control.

250. What is more laughable than a skinny little animal that thus snarls, enkindling blackest tragedies!— and for things of no value.

251. Sometimes this is for gifts of the body, or of Fortune, or even—if the gods allow—for one little word!

252. You shall easily subdue anger if you hold and fasten this in your mind.

253. No injury should be done, except if your soul were to be harmed—and this, no man can do except its possessor, by introducing it to sin.

254. We have spoken hitherto of things coming from man and going to man: we will now discuss higher matters, as coming from God. The former matters were of God also, but these that follow are even more expressly so.

ON RELIGION

255. Nothing greater or more excellent can be given to man than religion, which is the knowledge, love, and veneration of the Prince and Father of this world.

256. Unto no other people is God so beneficent, especially to those to whom He teaches the truths of His cult.

257. Therefore, the Psalmist proposes this one gift high-

est among all those given to the people of Israel: "It is He Who announces His word unto Jacob, His justice and His judgments to Israel."

258. "He has not done so to every nation, nor has He manifested His judgments to them."

259. God is made known through religion: and being known, He must of necessity be loved and worshipped.

260. God alone is Prince and Author and Lord of the Universe, Who alone can do all things and knows all things.

261. This world is like His house or, better, His temple. This He brought forth out of nothing, fashioning and ornamenting it (hence known by the Greek word for ornament, *cosmos—mundus* in Latin— both meaning a beautiful ornament).

262. This world He so rules and governs that we may no less wonder at its conservation than at its creation.

263. Just as in the house of a most prudent head of the household, nothing is done without his orders; so in this world nothing is done without His will and bidding. He Who is omnipotent and omniscient knows all things.

264. Angels, devils, men, all living things, sticks and stones, the heavens and the elements—in short, all things—are governed by Him and obey Him.

265. There is nothing made, nothing that moves, nothing that changes, not the chaff which rises from the ground, not even a feather, that may act outside His precepts and commandments.

266. This is the law of the universe; there is no other chance or fortune or lot.

267. He does all things with highest equity and wisdom, even though these are ways unknown to us.

268. Whatever happens to any man, if he is good, turns to his profit—not to the profit of small moneys or of the transitory things of the world, but to eternal felicity.

269. Whatever things happen, then, must be received with equanimity and acknowledged as coming from God the Author, lest we with our passions and foolish judgment seem to condemn the will of that most righteous and wise governor of all things, God, whom no one can comprehend.

270. Although we are not able to encompass His purposes, it is right and just for us to praise and commend what He does.

271. Like children ignorant of what is best for us, we lament that things most harmful are not given us, judging them to be most useful. On the other hand, we stand quivering in fear before things we hold most profitable which, actually, are most hurtful.

272. Often, nothing more damnable can happen to us than that we obtain our own desires.

273. Since we are so surrounded by this great darkness of ignorance, it is God's will that the fault should be left to us alone and that we commit all the rest to His care.

274. We must execute, whether we will or no, the work which the Governor of this great world has commanded and appointed for us. Therefore, why be

drawn against our will, with weeping and wailing, rather than follow merrily and willingly?

275. Truly, every friend of God will gladly obey the laws of His Friend.

276. This is the highest manner of loving God; as Christ says, "You shall be my friends if you will do what I have commanded you."

ON CHRIST

277. The Reconciler of mankind with God and Author of our salvation is Jesus Christ, true man and true God, the only son of God Almighty. Him the Father sent for that purpose when it pleased Him to take pity on mankind which had made itself, to its own great hurt, an enemy of God, His Father and Creator.

278. No evil can be conceived more hurtful or destructive than by sin to be separated from God, the fountain of all continuing goodness, and to be turned to most pernicious misery; or to be taken from a most sweet life, and left to a most bitter death.

279. For this purpose among others, Christ came that He might lead us in the straightest way on which we might steadfastly chart our journey God-ward, not swerving from it the breadth of a hair.

280. He has discovered to us, and pointed out, this way by His words; He has cleared it and made it safe by the example of His holy life.

281. All human wisdom compared with the Christian religion is but squalor and unmixed folly.

282. Much that is grave, prudent, wise, pure, holy, or

religious can be read in the books of the ancient pagan writers, much that merits admiration, exclamation, and applause. Whatever is in them is commended, learned by heart, and praised to the skies—yet all this is found more purely, more righteously, more openly, and more easily in our holy religion.

283. Perfect wisdom is to know this religion; perfect virtue is to live according to it. For no man knows it in truth who does not live it in deed.

284. Christ's life witnesses to His true humanity; His miracles attest to the omnipotence of His divinity; His law demonstrates His heavenly wisdom.

285. Hence, of His perfect life, we have an example to follow; of His authority, strength to obey; of His wisdom, faith to believe.

286. Goodness arouses love; majesty promotes worship; wisdom engenders faith.

287. If a man carefully considers those things which Christ commands, he shall find that everything redounds to his benefit, so that no one feels that he entrusts himself to Him except for his own greatest good.

288. Nothing is more pleasant to man than to be trusted for himself; so it is with God. No one thinks well of that man to whom he reluctantly entrusts himself.

289. The foundation of our salvation is to believe God to be the Father; and Jesus Christ, His only Son, to be our lawgiver; and the Holy Spirit to be breathed out of them both. Without God we can do nothing, nor can we think anything noble or profitable.

290. The true worshipping of God is to purge completely from the soul all diseases and depraved passions; thereby we can be transformed as closely to His resemblance as is possible, to be pure and holy as He is. Like Him, we will hate no man, but rather we will work zealously to be useful to all men.

291. The more you transfer yourself from things of the body to things of the soul, the more God-like a life you shall lead.

292. Thus it will happen that God acknowledges our nature to be like His: He will delight in it, making it His own true and genuine temple, much more acceptable to Him than churches made of stone and metals.

293. As Paul says, "You are the temple of God."

294. Such a noble guest must be retained: He must not be expelled through the fetidness of sins.

295. Corporal works are tasteless before God unless seasoning be added from the heart.

296. You should realize that you have God in the innermost recess of your very heart and soul, far from every eye, as witness and judge of all your thoughts. If you fear His presence, you will not only avoid doing evil, but you will also not admit to your soul anything unclean or sinful.

297. Love of God ought to be such that you hold Him above all other things and that His honor and glory are dearer to you than all the dignities and honors of this life.

298. When one friend remembers another, he is moved with a cordial and tender joy; so let things divine

seem most lovable to you and so acceptable that you will turn to them with the greatest gladness.

299. Whenever you hear God spoken of, recall His works to be greater and more excellent than human knowledge can conceive.

300. Listen to what is spoken of Him and of His saints, not as you do for things of men, but with great wonderment of mind.

301. Do not judge God lightly, nor pronounce judgment on His works except with reverence and fear.

302. It would be impious to jest about holy things, or scoffingly to twist the sayings of Holy Scripture into foolish word-games and trifling tales. This would be like a man sprinkling dirt into a medicine designed for the recovery of health, but applying Scripture to obscenities is completely nefarious and intolerable.

303. Rather, all things are to be marveled at, and should be received with worthy reverence into our souls.

304. Participate in religious exercises attentively and piously. Thus, whatever you see or hear there will appear most pure and sacrosanct and pertinent to God's majesty, which is at once easy to worship and impossible to comprehend.

305. Thus, these things are always hidden in that divine wisdom which is higher than the strength and penetration of man's mind is able to reach.

306. We reverence the hidden sayings of wise men, although we do not understand them. Then why should we not defer equally to God's?

307. As often as you hear Jesus Christ named, let it recall to mind His inestimable love toward us; let

this remembrance of His name be to you full of sweetness and veneration.

308. When you hear any title, or pithy description, made of Christ, lift yourself up in contemplation of it, praying that He will show Himself even such a one toward you. Thus, when you hear Him called merciful, meek, or gentle, pray that He will prove the same to you. When He is called almighty, pray that He may show it in restoring you from the most wretched conditions to the best; from an enemy, to His son; from nothing, to something. When He is called terrible, pray that He may terrify those of whom you are afraid.

309. When you call Him Lord, see that you serve Him; when you call Him Father, see that you love Him, showing yourself worthy to be the son of such a Father.

310. Nothing in all the universe exists whose origin, nature, and power, when beheld, do not furnish you matter to praise or worship God, the Author of all things.

311. Begin nothing without first recalling the presence of God; for He in Whose hands are both progress and decline gives prosperous furtherance to such acts as we deliberately begin in that manner.

312. Whatever you begin, have an eye to its outcome; yet when you have made a right intention, do not be solicitous for the results.

313. Have faith that in His power rests the success of all things.

314. All religious sentiments are hidden in the heart's intimacy. Make an effort to comprehend intelli-

gently what you pray, not losing time in lip service. When you pray, let your soul and mind, your intellect and will agree together in gestures so that these work in harmony and respond to that most excellent action.

315. The sacred axiom condemns him who says the divine office negligently.

316. If it be a shame for a minstrel to sing one thing and to play another not harmonious with what he sings, it is much more shame for us when singing the psalms of God to speak one thing with the tongue, and think another in our soul.

317. Let our desires be sober and worthy of being aired before God, and then answered, rather than offensive through their folly and impropriety.

ON THE CONSUMPTION OF FOOD

318. When you are about to dine, recall the infinite power of God Who made all things from nothing. Recall His wisdom and benignity which sustain the same; and finally, call to mind His gentleness and clemency which cherish even His extreme enemies.

319. Ponder how great a thing it is daily to prepare varieties of foods for all the peoples of the whole world; what a thing it is to conserve all things, keeping them from that nothingness into which they tend by their own inclination.

320. No wisdom of man nor of angel is able in any wise to perform this thing, nor even to understand it.

321. Inasmuch as you know that you exist because of His goodness, consider what accursed ingratitude, and what damnable rashness it is, to dare to be at

odds with Him by Whose benefit and will you have your being. You would have no future, if He did not will it.

322. At your table, let all things be chaste, pure, wise, and holy, even as He is, Whose gifts you now have in hand.

323. Let all backbiting, bitterness, outrage, and cruelty be sequestered far from your table where you sense, rather, the incredible sweetness and clemency of God toward you.

324. It is the more intolerable that you should contaminate a place with sharpness and hatred against your brother, where you discover such benign and open-handed gifts dispensed toward you.

325. This fact the classical pagan writers well perceived because they called sacred the table which was joyful and festive. They counted it criminal if any sad or heinous matter was said or done there.

326. You have God Who is highest in might, wisdom, and liberality to sustain you in your concerns, the while He dispenses only His gifts. Put away the inordinate regard for yourself wherein you seem to mistrust His goodness. Have for your only care how you may please Him and serve Him the more.

327. It is a great foolishness to admit any contention to your table, for you to displease Him from Whom all nourishment comes; it is a madness to call down the displeasure of one from Whom you petition your requests so earnestly.

328. This life is particularly not preserved by nourishment but by the will of God; according to the

saying of Scripture, "Not in bread alone does man live, but by the word of God."

329. We have the guarantee of Jesus, Lord of all in heaven and on earth, that they shall lack nothing who seek the kingdom of God and His justice.

330. Seeing, therefore, that God is so bountiful toward you in His gifts, you should be as kind to your brother, accounting him without envy to be no less the son of God than yourself. God is no more bound to you than to him. He has only wanted you to be a minister and dispenser of His gifts, from whom, after God, your brother should be able to ask assistance.

331. Nothing is more truly given to Christ than that which is given to the poor.

332. When you have eaten food and drink, consider Whose wisdom and power it is which sustains and supports the life given us.

333. Give thanks, therefore, to God, not as you would to one who has prepared sustenance for you with his money—but such thanks as are proper for Him Who has made both you and the food for you, sustaining you and it, not through the latter's strength of itself, but by His will.

ON SLEEP

334. At your retiring and your rising, recall the benefits of God, not only toward you but to all mankind, and to all the whole world.

335. Consider how many insidious enemies of man alight upon him in his sleep while he lies like a corpse

having no power of himself; Christ must so much the more unremittingly be sought that He will defend us weaklings.

336. Nor should we let our sins provoke to anger our Protector and our Ruler.

337. On the exterior, arm your forehead and your breast with the Sign of the Cross; in the secret part of your heart, with devout prayers and holy meditations.

338. When you go to bed, reflect on the way each day resembles the whole life of man. Night succeeds the day, just as sleep is a most expressive figure of death.

339. We must, therefore, beg Christ that in life and in death He be always with us, propitious and kind, just as in this night He will grant us peace and tranquility, and freedom from the terror of nightmares.

340. Even in sleeping, we may have Him in mind. Thus, refreshed with His comfort, we may rise merrily in the morning, while yet remembering His most precious death, the price whereby He redeemed mankind.

341. You should keep your bed chaste and pure, so that your enemy, the author and source of all defilement, may not enter.

342. With the Sign of the Cross, holy water, and the invocation of the Name of God, but primarily with holy thoughts and firm resolution toward holiness, you will repel the power of the fiends from there.

343. When you rise in the morning, commit yourself to Christ, rendering thanks to Him, that through His

help and defense He has preserved you that night from the deceits and envy of that monstrous enemy.

344. As you have first slept the night-time and are now risen again, so remember that our bodies, having first slept through death, will afterwards be restored to life by Christ when He shall appear to judge both the living and the dead.

345. Humbly beseech Him that it may be His will that you spend the day following in His service, neither injuring nor being injured by any man; that, enclosed on every side and fortified with Christian piety, you may safely escape the nets and snares which the devil, most deceitful enemy, never ceases to spread out for mankind in all our ways and passages.

346. Venerate Mary, the Most Blessed Mother of God, and other holy saints, the dearly beloved friends of Christ dwelling with Him in eternity.

347. Read, and listen most attentively to the lives and acts of the saints that you, being piously and prayerfully animated, may imitate them.

348. Regard and speak about them, not as of ordinary men, but as of those who transcended all nature and human excellence and are now united and conjoined to God.

ON CHARITY

349. A great likeness among men can be observed in body and mind, for we all have been brought into this world under the same jurisdiction, made for a common society of life. For the latter's preservation,

Nature has proclaimed this law, "Let no man do to another what he does not want done to himself."

350. He Who restored our fallen nature has professed this one doctrine to be His, both explicating and illustrating it Himself.

351. In order that He might elevate human nature to the likeness of God up to the highest point possible, He commanded us not only to love one another, but also to love those who hate us.

352. Thus, we will be like the Father of heaven Who sincerely loves His enemies, as He declares by His many benefits pursuing them. He hates no one whatever.

353. Such is the condition of men that they want others to bear good will to them, even those whom they resent.

354. That most wise Master and Author of our life has given us this one instruction for living: that is, to love one another. By this rule, we might skillfully lead a most blessed life, without need of any other law.

355. Nothing is more blessed than to love: therefore, God and His angels, who love all things, are most blessed.

356. Nothing is more wretched than to hate: for which reason the devils are most miserable.

357. True love balances everything equally. Where it thrives, no man seeks preferment. No man robs someone he loves, by accounting things to be his which are his friend's. Love contends not with his dear brother, nor does he think himself afflicted with any injury by him.

358. No man rejoices in the misfortunes of his friend, neither is he grieved at his prosperity; contrariwise, he rejoices with those who rejoice and weeps with those who weep, according to the saying of the Apostle—and this he does not do falsely or hypocritically, but with all his heart. Love holds all things in common; so he esteems those things which pertain to the beloved as though his own.

359. These enduring lessons, and the truest example of them set before our eyes for imitation, are found in the life and works of Christ.

360. The Son of God came to teach us the right way of living, not only in word but by example of life. Our hearts being thus illuminated by that clear sunbeam of His teaching, we may discern clearly what things really are.

361. When from the first He was exercised in every kind of patience, what moderation of soul did He not show, notwithstanding His infinite power and might. When assaulted with grievous injuries, He never spoke back an evil word: thus He taught this only way to God, by abhorring the contrary. He suffered Himself to be bound Who might have overturned the whole world with a single nod of the head.

362. How patiently He suffered calumny!

363. Finally, He so bore Himself that no man could perceive in Him any power except to succor others.

364. The King and Lord of all, by Whom the Father made this world, how calmly He bore Himself when He was equated with the weakest men, and when He had neither house for Himself, nor sustenance for His beloved disciples.

365. The Creator and Governor of Nature was not exempt from the ills of our nature. He hungered, He thirsted, He was weary, and He mourned: these infirmities He suffered for our example.

366. So great a friend was He to peace, concord, and charity that He pursued no sin more than pride, and others springing from it: arrogance, ambition, contention, strivings, and grudges.

367. Thus he showed that there is nothing which a man should arrogate to himself by reason of any outward or bodily gift which is accidental and alien to him; nor again, of the inward powers of man, or of his virtue.

368. For these are given by—and cherished on account of—God. No man should advance himself for such gifts, or forget their source and origin, or despise those men for whose aid he had received his endowment from God.

369. And to shatter this pride, and to assure that no man would be conceited (though he had complied in every rite of religion and fully observed the law of the Gospel), we have heard Him speak thus, "When you have done all I commanded you, say that we are but unprofitable servants."

370. How foolish are they who glory in their exact Christianity, preferring themselves before all others as observers of the Law!

371. Often he whom you think very hated of God, in comparison with yourself, is richer in virtue than you and destined for the comforts of heaven, when you shall be appointed to eternal miseries!

372. Therefore, God, reserving the scrutinizing knowledge of hearts only to Himself, has removed from

man all judging of man, for the one is blind and ignorant of the secrets of the other's heart.

373. The outward things which only the eye of man beholds are but weak and uncertain signs of inward secrets.

374. Hence, one should not pass judgment concerning any man's intention, vice, or virtue, merely for having been once in his company, not even a hundred times, nor a lifetime.

375. Most deep and dark are the hidden dens of man's heart: whose sight is sharp enough to pierce through such a great darkness?

376. And seeing that Christ in dying has redeemed all mankind with such a great price from the servitude of the devil, let no man dare to contemn or play sport with his own soul. It was this which the Lord so entirely loved that He did not shrink from pouring out His own blood and exchanging His life for it.

377. The Lord was crucified for all of us, and for each of us.

378. Do not hope for the grace of Christ if you hate the one whom He loves.

379. He requires no other thanks but that we love our fellow-servants, as He, being Our Lord, loved us when we were evil and sinful and deserving of punishment.

380. Here He instituted that mutual bond of love between man and man, and between man and God— that is to say, the foundation of man's felicity which culminates in Heaven.

381. This is the life and grace of Christ, His wisdom

exceeding man's intelligence, His justice satisfying those who understand, and His goodness alluring all men.

382. Let no man impute himself to be a Christian, or trust that he is in the favor of God if he hate anyone, since Christ has commended all men to our love.

383. Since man has been so commended by God, love each one who deserves it because he whom you love is worthy: if he does not deserve it, love him because God Whom you obey is worthy.

384. Neither fasting nor great riches bestowed upon the poor render a man acceptable to God. Only charity toward man brings this to pass, as that Apostle has taught us.

385. You ought to see each man as your natural brother, rejoicing in his prosperity and sorrowing for his adversity, assisting him as much as you can.

386. Let not love of nation, or of city, or of kindred diminish this affection—nor of profession, or state of life, or wit. For there is one Father of all, God, Whom you are taught by Christ each day to call Father. He will acknowledge you to be His son if you acknowledge all His sons to be your brothers.

387. Be not embarrassed to take him for your brother whom God does not disdain to take for His son.

388. God introduced us to peace, concord, and love.

389. The devil (that most expert schemer) invented parties, factions, private profits, and other damning actions such as dissensions, brawls, contentions, and wars.

390. God, willing our salvation, sows among us benev-

olence; the devil, willing our destruction sows enmities.

391. Fellowship unites in small issues; discord dissipates in great concerns.

392. They who study to bring peace among men, and to preserve tranquility safe and sound, shall be called the children of God, as Christ testifies. These are the true peacemakers of whom He spoke. Contrarily, those who sow discord and destroy charity among men are sons of the devil.

393. The greatest enmity, in which man surpasses the ferocity of wild animals, is war, a matter of inhumanity which is best described by the term "beastly."

394. How Nature herself abhors war! For she brought forth man into this world unarmed, and shaped him to meekness and to sociability. God also abhors the same, for He willed and commanded mutual love between man and man.

395. Man cannot war against man, nor harm another, without serious offense.

396. If you suspect any man to bear a grudge or displeasure in his mind toward you, avoid no labor or toil to reconcile and pacify him.

397. In this behalf, do not spare yourself in prayers, service, or fortune: by so doing you will attain to the esteem of men, that swift road to the esteem of God.

398. Scoff at no man, remembering that whatsoever chances to one may as well happen to another. Rather give thanks to God that He has kept you from such misfortunes; and pray, partly that no

such accident occur to you; and partly that there be a remedy for the afflicted one, or at least for his equanimity of soul. Then help him, if you are able to do so.

399. It is a cruel spirit which rejoices in another man's misfortune, refusing to commiserate in our common nature.

400. Be merciful to man, and God will have mercy on you.

401. The fate and tragedy that follow mankind are common to all, threatening each and all, hanging over each and all.

402. Owing man such love, then, know that you can do nothing more appropriate or agreeable than to procure for him that highest good, virtue. Even if you were to study to be able to do all things, you could still not render a greater good.

403. Likewise, you can do nothing more jarring, more damnable, or more deterrent to this love than to bring man to sin through persuasion, or example, or any other incitement.

404. The highest and happiest of all things is for a man to love, even though he is unloved; but most joyful of all is, while loving, to be himself loved entirely.

405. No treasure is more certain than sure friendship.

406. No guard is so strong as faithful friends.

407. He takes the sun from out of the world, who takes friendship from life.

408. True love, and solid, stable friendship rest only in those who are virtuous: among these, love easily builds up.

409. Evil men are neither friends among themselves, nor with the good.

410. The fastest and surest way to be loved is first to love: love is allured by nothing so much as love.

411. Love is acquired also by Virtue: her nature is so lovable that often she invites to love and, in a manner, constrains men who never knew her.

412. Love is also enticed by signs of virtue, such as meekness, sympathy, modesty, courtesy, and affable gentleness; or signs whereby you do or say nothing which savors of arrogance, insolence, petulance, or ribaldry. Everything should be sweet, soft, gentle, and pure.

413. It is the poison of friendship to love as though you disdain your friend, or so to hold him as to impute him your enemy.

414. This is a wholesome saying, "Hate as though you loved."

415. Let no thought of enmity enter where friendship is; do not presume that your present friend will never be your future enemy (otherwise your friendship is very weak and fragile).

416. In friendship there must be such faith, constancy, and simplicity that in no wise would you have any suspicions, or give ear to any who suspect or accuse your friend.

417. Life is no life to those who live in suspicion and fear; rather, it is a continual death.

418. Do not inquire into others' lives nor seek evil in the house of the just, as the Book of Wisdom says. Nor scrutinize curiously what each does; fear above all that you should discover any turpitude or

wish to know it. For this is the act of an inhuman heart, and a bitter spirit; and many grudges will rise hence.

419. Those who do such things are accustomed to be careless about their own affairs but are solicitous about other men's affairs, being unduly curious about them. It is folly to know other men well, and not to know yourself at all.

HOW ONE SHOULD LIVE WITH MEN

420. Not only should you love all men like this, but also reverence equally those who are your equals, honestly and decorously behaving yourself among them as required by the duty of your social life.

421. Do not think that it makes no difference where, and with whom, and in whose company you do or speak anything.

422. When you are among others, so discipline the parts of your body—and especially your eyes and countenance—that there may be no sign of disdain or contempt. Use no wanton gestures. Let there be present only that quietness and serenity which prove the control of the soul's passions.

423. The first and most beautiful garment of man's face is modesty and humility without which the countenance seems deformed and detestable.

424. All hope of recovery is past in him who is no longer embarrassed at evil-doing.

425. Do not show too much severity or grimness in your face, for thereby men presume the mind to be cruel and unruly.

426. Do not laugh too frequently, immoderately, or loudly, nor let your body shake withal, nor permit an outburst of derision.

427. Nothing can make you merrier than to have a good laugh.

428. There may be some cause for laughter, but never for an outburst.

429. To laugh at the good is wicked; at the evil, cruelty; at the indifferent, madness; at the upright, an impiety; at the wicked, a barbarity; at those whom we know, a monstrosity; at those unknown, derangement. In short, to make fun of man is inhuman.

430. Let your eyes be quiet and your hands steady, not nervous or gesticulating. Do not play games with your hands.

431. After a snap of the fingers there follows a blow of the fist—and after that there follow clubs and swords.

432. Give to truly good men that brotherly respect which is born from a veneration for the soul.

433. Give the most profound honor to those who are in authority; obey them, even if they command burdensome and troublesome things—God wills this so, for the public peace.

434. Give way to the wealthy, lest being stirred to anger, they injure both you and other good men, too.

435. Rise for your elders; reverence age as that in which is often found great experience and knowledge of living. At the honor which others give you, do not begrudge returning an equal honor. It is a great

rudeness not to salute him who salutes you; a point of extreme barbarism, not to wish well to him who wishes well to you. What small things and of what slight cost are salutations, gentle speech, kindness, and reverence! What great friendship do they engender if they are manifest; or dissolve, if omitted! What ignorance of what is right for us, not to wish to gain the good will of many men with such a small trifle costing so little! The more refined a man is, the higher his education, the more humbly and courteously he behaves himself; the lower his background, the more disdainful and curt he is, sometimes from ignorance—hence, learning in the gracious arts is called "humanities." If you salute and are not saluted in return, ascribe it to carelessness or distraction rather than to premeditated contempt. If you are addressed with too few courtesies and honorary titles, attribute it to a man's lack of good manners, or to habit, and not to malice or hatred. Do not be so petty as to be moved with the breath of a man's mouth. By such interpretations, and others similar, you shall lead a holy life, filled with joy: for you shall love every man, and never judge yourself offended or hurt by one person. There is an old proverb: "To be true, be not suspicious." These following words may be new, but the moral is old: "To be serene, be not suspicious."

436. See to it that you show no contempt of any man in countenance, word, or deed.

437. If you, being of low degree, contemn your superiors, how will your inferiors act toward you? If you are of the higher rank, by your proud contempt you turn your subordinates from you.

438. Contempt is an intolerable thing for no man considers himself so vile that he deserves it.

439. Many persons labor to justify themselves in their contempt; but more plot how to be revenged.

440. There is no man so great but Fortune may bring him to beg the help of the poorest and seek succor of the lowest.

441. Beside all this, no man is contemptible whom God considers worthy to take for His son: hence, you contemn God's judgment in such a person.

442. Often, men, once considered worthy of contempt, upon investigation are found to be most worthy of reverence and respect.

ON SPEECH AND COMMUNICATION

443. God gave man a tongue to be an instrument of communication in society, in which Nature binds man to man.

444. This tongue is the cause of great benefits and mischiefs, depending on its use. Therefore, James, the Apostle, compares it properly to the rudder of a ship. Roping must be thrown on it and drawn tight, so that it neither hurts others, nor itself.

445. Sin is wrought by no instrument so easily, nor so often, as by the tongue.

446. You should make fun of no man, curse no man, injure no man in any manner, nor his business, reputation, or good name.

447. You should not abusively nor scornfully rage like a wild man against anyone, even if you are provoked or driven to it. In doing so, you hurt yourself more

before God and men of wisdom than him against whom you rail.

448. To exchange one evil word for another is to clean mud with mud.

449. Threatening loudly is for harlots, not for the virtuous.

450. Do not be of so weak a mind and tender a heart that a few words are able to wound you.

451. Do not use snappish words nor biting sarcasm if you want to appear an eloquent speaker. Toward another's affronts, it would be better to be as children or as mutes.

452. Do not be solicitous about censuring others; take care, rather, that they find nothing in you to censure.

453. If perchance you rebuke a person, do not use sharp or bitter words; in the bitterness mingle some sweetness to temper the bitter chiding. Thereby, you assuage the wound, even if you cut deeply.

454. Furthermore, do not lose the fruit of your reprimand in your earnest effort to mitigate the matter —nor should you slide into mere flattery.

455. Soothing flattery is a deforming vice, bringing the sayer to dishonesty and the hearer to great harm.

456. Evaluate nothing so precious that you would swerve from right and truth. Let neither riches or necessities, nor entreaty or threatenings, nor fear of death or certain danger, wrench you away.

457. In doing so, whatever you say shall have the authority of Gospels and faith; contrariwise, you would be judged despicable and unworthy to be heard.

458. Let your speech be modest, civil, gentle, neither rough or countrified, nor overbearing or excessively exact and affected (lest one should need an interpreter to understand you).

459. At no time use contumelious, reprehensible, or threatening language, nor words flattering, minced, and fawning.

460. A man can reach a certain balance which neither denies his own dignity nor takes away another's.

461. Wantonness and defilement should be extirpated from your speech, as poison is from food.

462. Do not be hasty when you speak, nor let your tongue precede your thought. Make no answer before you perfectly understand what the matter means about which you are asked and what was said, and what he felt to whom you reply.

463. This saying, "Tell me everything which comes to your lips"—a thing which Cicero asked only of Atticus—ought seldom to be applied. I do not even know if it should be admitted in any case, since even among friends we ought to be on our guard about not saying any light thing which might dissolve or offend friendship.

464. So evil and so damaging, O Tongue, whither do you go?

465. Christ our Lord knew the evils which spring from loquacity and which work against the principal parts of His law, such as quarrels, discords, and grudges.

466. Consequently, He warned men to be circumspect in their speech—for every idle word they have spoken, they will have to make an account at the day of judgment.

467. Additionally, the Psalmist says, "Set a watch to my mouth, and a gate of circumspection before my lips."

468. Guard against being too busy in talking, or too full of words; nor should you wish people to listen to you alone. There is a certain procedure in talking, even with most unlearned or ordinary persons. Do not be so deliberate and slow-speaking that it seems you listen only to yourself—and perhaps, actually do so. Otherwise, you give the impression that each single word is for you like a unique rose.

469. Among wise men, it is better for you to listen than to speak. Yet it can happen that to be silent is as great a fault as it is to speak at an unpropitious time. No pleasure or enjoyment can be compared to discourse with a man who is wise and learned.

470. Let no one be unduly inquisitive, for this can cause pain and harm. You know what Horace says, "Fly from the busybody: such a one is commonly a babbler."

471. Do not be contentious or obstinate in argument. When you hear the truth, reverence it immediately with silence, rising as though to a godly thing.

472. Even if you hear something unreasonable, overlook it through your friendliness and modesty, especially when right living and piety are not offended.

473. Contention is pointless where there is no hope of progress.

474. Men can scarcely tolerate arrogance, boastfulness, or fastidious superiority, not even in great men deserving of highest praise.

475. Not in words but in deeds will your knowledge be proclaimed.

476. Do not think that other men delight to hear what you enjoy saying.

477. Take care that you do nothing which would make you uneasy if it is not concealed. If, however, you have done any such thing, disclose it to no one else —or if it must be told, look carefully to whom you tell it. When committing anything of counsel to your friend which you wish kept secret, be careful that you use no manner of joking, lest later in repeating the jest he reveal your secret.

478. Like a true trust, keep the secret committed to your custody more precisely and more faithfully than money deposited with you.

479. Nothing would be safe in man's life if loyalty to secrets were overthrown.

480. If you promise anything, keep your word, no matter how hard and difficult it may be for you, so that at least you will fulfill the word which you gave.

481. If anything is promised to you, do not demand it; but be more exacting a judge of yourself than of others.

482. It must be obvious to you that men have their senses, reason, intelligence, and judgment. Do not hope that you would be able to persuade them to take evil deeds for good, or to be deceived by things counterfeited, cloaked, disguised, or copied. These ultimately betray themselves: the more skillfully they were hidden, the more evil and insidious they are.

483. For our minds are indeed aroused to hostility against those things in which we have been deceived.

484. So, it is better that all things be open, uncloaked, and single-minded.

485. Although truth sometimes displeases in the beginning, there is finally nothing more amiable and gracious.

486. Truth may well suffer, but it will never be overcome.

487. The advantage from lying is neither solid nor durable; neither is the damage done by truthfulness.

488. Despise lying as common rottenness. There is no more abject condition in man than lying, in which way we separate ourselves from God and become like the devil, and become his bondsman.

489. Finally, sooner or later, deceitfulness is discovered, and returns to the disgrace of the one who uttered it.

490. What is despised more, what more vicious, than a liar?

491. Once you are known to be a liar, no man will believe you, even though you affirm the most truthful things.

492. Contrariwise, if you are true of word, your nod of the head shall be better believed than the most sacred oaths of other men.

493. If you speak nothing contrary, and if your words agree with one another, you will not need the effort of memory, or any other art, except always to speak what you know to be true.

494. Truth always coincides with truth; falsehood, neither with truth nor with other falsehood.

495. If you wish your opinions to be accepted as true,

accept nothing lightly but what is assuredly known or else has a great likelihood for verisimilitude.

496. Nor should you be suspicious, according to the wise saying, "If you wish to be truthful, do not be suspicious."

497. He is in misery who so acts that he is unable to extricate himself from his entanglements except by more lying.

ABOUT OATHS

498. Do not become accustomed to swearing; for the Wise Man says, "He who swears much will be filled with wickedness, and the plague shall not recede from his house."

499. Christ in His Gospel forbids us to swear; affirming, we should say only, "yes, yes"; or denying, say only "nay, nay."

500. Great reverence is due to God. He ought not to be called indiscriminately as witness, in every place for every trifle. No, we ought never to swear by Him unless we are obliged or compelled to do so.

501. He who swears easily in true matters will swear also in jest; he who swears in jest will swear in lies.

502. They who believe you will as well believe you with or without an oath; they who will not believe you disdain your most solemn oath.

ON HOW TO HANDLE MEN

503. Among men there is a certain difference to be discriminated: some are one's own family, some are only acquaintances, and some are strangers.

504. I call "one's own family" those who are of kinship or of affinity, or with whom you live together in one home and household.

505. You must love all men. So behave yourself toward strangers that even they whom you do not know may perceive you to be a friend universally to all mankind, wishing well to all.

506. And yet, you should not be as a white line upon a white stone, showing yourself alike to all men. Some you should admit to counsel; to some, be obedient; some you shall reverence with honor; and to some you should render thanks, if you have received any benefits at their hands or, more importantly, if you have profited from their diligent and faithful service.

507. A man's good will is to be judged by his deeds. A man wanting, and trying, to do well is but one step lower than he who actually did well.

508. He who has received a benefit is no less bound to pay back or recompense solicitously than one who has borrowed money.

509. He would be considered of no less good will who has given of his thoughtfulness, than he who gives his money. Even more than the preceding, it is only logical that the body is judged dearer to a man than any thing extrinsic. Do not wait until your friend tells you of his needs, but smell them out yourself, succoring him of your own accord. Meet an honest request beforehand—before it is asked, answer it.

510. You shall not only love your parents but also venerate them next to God; you shall be obedient to their commands as though they were from on high.

511. Be thoroughly persuaded that they are in God's

stead for you here on earth, and that no man loves you more entirely, nor has greater care for you.

512. Next to them are schoolmasters, pedagogues, tutors, and all who have been entrusted with your instruction in conduct; they are of such great value that man can possess nothing more precious or more excellent.

513. Love and reverence teachers as if they were your second parents. With humility and alacrity obey them, counting whatever they tell you as not for their benefit but for yours.

514. Since this is the case, you would make slender recompense if for such kindness or such efforts for your benefit, you would respond with hatred or obstinate disobedience.

515. Believe that he cherishes you tenderly who reprehends you lovingly.

516. He rarely hurts you who reproves you even if he be your enemy: for if he speaks truthfully, he shows you what to reform—if falsely, he teaches you what to avoid. Thus, in any event, he makes you the better or, at least, more circumspect.

517. When you are about to make some individuals your close friends, first search out their manner of life. Inquire how they conduct themselves with their other friends, so that afterwards you may not regret such an acquaintance.

518. Refuse a relationship with him whose familiarity you see honest men to eschew. Likewise, shun those whom you perceive to love your goods, not you yourself; for these are parasites by whose conversation you may either wear worse, or fall into danger

and peril. Shun all who envy their friends' fortune. Studiously avoid, as friends, those who have no serious thought in life, who loudly jest at the secrets of their friends and tell jokes about them. Through innate loquaciousness they pour out what should, with exquisite concern, be kept reticently. Most of all, avoid those who for a trifle would be at utter defiance with their best friend, revenging themselves more upon those whom they once loved than on those whom they always hated. Unthinkingly, they persuade themselves that the injury done to a friend is less intolerable than the injury done to an enemy. In so doing, they plainly declare that they never loved in the first place; for if they had, they would never have thought themselves offended so soon. It were better to consider such persons as enemies and strangers, than friends.

519. Take care in making a friend; be doubly assiduous in retaining him.

520. Choose a close friend who will not only please you, but will make you better. Avoid him who will say everything for your pleasure. Rather than him who speaks only in commendation, embrace one who will truthfully admonish you for your faults.

521. If you take delight in listening to those who flatter you, you shall never hear the truth.

522. Among beastly passions, the most forward is envy; among the most timid, flattery.

523. Wisdom and virtue are worthy of all men's love: flattery ought to be curbed, since the latter impedes our coming to the former by persuading us that we have already obtained them. Moreover, plain ad-

monition does more than a little good because it
brings a man to virtue by teaching him what remains yet behind, and how it must be brought forward.

524. If it grieves you to be reprehended, do nothing reprehensible.

525. He is in a miserable situation who, needing a friend
to admonish him, has none.

526. Flee from the company of evil men as from men
infected with the plague; contagion from the one
is to be feared no less than from the other.

527. The exception would be if you yourself were able
to make them better.

528. Yet you must not trust yourself therein with too
much confidence: remember that as our nature of
itself is prone to evil, so also the sloping road to
virtue is very steep.

529. Ask yourself who you are, what degree and status
you have, and do not presume that things are more
lawful for you than for other men.

530. The more that custom makes lawful, the more
should moderation restrain us from putting these
concessions to use.

531. Be gentle to your inferiors, respectful to your bet-
ters, easy and tractable to your peers.

532. Nevertheless, always be hard, stiff, and inexorable
to vice.

533. Bear with being contemned unjustly by those more
powerful; judge the situation to have come more
by the course of bad fortune than by the fault of
men.

534. If anything which displeases you be done to you by your social inferiors, do not consider it done from contempt but rather from a freedom of restraint.

535. Reckon yourself very delicate if you count small ticklings to be great blows.

536. You must not suppose only yourself a man, and other men beasts who must remain mute. You are a man; live as other men do, under the same law.

537. If you are really a wiser and better person than other men, you will be indulgent toward them. Concede every point of the law to them, as to men less learned and strong. Do not cloak over ignorance in yourself, whom wisdom and virtue have presumably strengthened.

538. If you do not excel in virtue, why do you demand higher esteem than others? If you excel others, why do you not moderate your passions any better than the common people?

539. It is better to accept injury than to give it, better to be deceived than to deceive. This human wisdom was understood by men such as Socrates, Plato, Aristotle, and Seneca.

540. It is human fragility to err through being deceived. Hence, do not permit other men's offenses, especially those done against yourself, to offend you greatly.

541. A gentle and noble heart forgives; a cruel, beastly, unnatural, and evil heart holds its anger, something which Nature exhibits even in dumb animals.

542. Since God does nothing more often, or more gladly, than to forgive, who is so demented as to deny that the same thing is at once most beautiful and most

excellent in us who resemble so closely the nature of the high and almighty God?

543. Be to other men as you wish Christ would be to you.

544. It is truly proper that you grant forgiveness to others who have done less to you, just as you need forgiveness from God's hands, either for the same or worse offenses.

545. No prayer is more acceptable, or more efficacious before God than the one taught us by His Son Christ, Our Lord, and for that reason called "The Lord's Prayer."

546. Now, you cannot really say that prayer in all honesty unless you completely forgive your brother from your heart, just as you pray God to forgive you.

547. A great debt is forgiven us, on this condition, that we remit a small debt.

548. Howsoever a man offends another, it is nothing in comparison with how any man whatever sins against God every single moment, which is so much more serious as God is greater and higher than man.

549. If you are angry with anyone, follow closely the counsel of the Apostle, "Let not the sun go down upon your wrath."

550. When you go to bed, cast out from your soul all quarrels, anger, unpleasantness, covetousness, and troubles. Your mind being quiet and settled, you may enjoy a tranquil sleep.

551. Let him whom you have once forgiven perceive your good will in action and that you yourself do not remember his insult, that he may experience

both your forgiveness of his injuries and now your friendliness, wherein you help him or give him some pleasure wherever possible.

552. Take care that you do not strike another in revenge, nor that you do vengeance to any other mortal. You have no authority over the servant of another, nor even over your fellow-servant. You insult your lord if you do not leave the correction of servants to him.

553. God is Lord over all men; we all are His servants. Be content to have complained to Him once. Rather, do not complain at all; for the eye of God sees all things and, as the Sacred Scripture testifies, He knows both him who does wrong and him who suffers it.

554. Therefore, He gave this commandment to everyone, "Leave revenge to me, and I will repay it."

555. Since the injury is in the intention and not in the deed, only God knows what moved the spirit and what punishment is owed there.

556. We often take for an injury that which is not; in doing so, we follow our passions which can by no means rightly examine the truth of the matter. Turned from that course, they are driven to judgments of their own.

ON MAN'S BEHAVIOR TOWARD HIMSELF

557. It behooves you not only to love yourself but also to show yourself worthy of being held in reverence. Thus, you should be embarrassed were you to go about doing anything unfit, imprudent, or impu-

dent, foul, scandalous, wicked, abominable, or impious.

558. Give more value to the judgment of your own conscience than to all the voices of the great multitude; for this latter is both unskilled and foolish, yet dares to approve and condemn matters it does not understand.

559. A troublesome conscience cruelly torments the soul; a quiet conscience brings supreme beatitude to which all worldly treasures and dignities cannot be compared.

560. It is this which the Lord promises in the Gospel to His disciples, that they shall receive even in this life more things than they have forsaken for His sake.

561. Fame shall neither profit the wicked person, nor hurt the good.

562. Once dead, what more profit shall you have of your fame than the famous picture of Apelles, or the victorious horse on Olympia? Fame little profits any man in his lifetime if he does not know about it; and if he knows it, what profit does it bring? A wise man will despise it, and a fool becomes more foolish because of it.

563. The witness of conscience is true, sound, and permanent, even more so when God shall sit in His dreadful judgment. Conscience is a great teacher. As the poet has wisely said, "Conscience is a bastion wall to stand between us and the innumerable dangers of this world." So secure is it that no terror can shake him whom this wall defends; for he is fastened and knit into God. He puts his trust in Him only, knowing that He whom the universe obeys has taken a peculiar charge of him.

564. It is deplorable for you to be known by others and unknown to yourself.

565. Is it not enough for you to be known by yourself and by God Who is supreme? Or do you, foolish one, seek a fuller theater, or a long-lasting name among other men?

566. They who cast away the regard of their good name and act audaciously and recklessly are doubly damnable; they do not reverence God, and they do not reverence man.

567. These injure their own conscience by deriding and deluding it. Presumably, they have despised reputation, claiming a liberty of conscience which now runs at large in sinfulness, unbridled with fear.

568. To love oneself is to essay, to work, to seek, and to strive with great prayers to God so that our most excellent part, the mind, might be adorned and cultivated with true brotherhood and ornaments, especially Religion.

569. He does not love himself who loves riches, or honors, or worldly pleasures or anything else extrinsic or corporal: for the most precious part of man is the mind.

570. Neither does he love himself who for lack of self-knowledge deceives himself, or permits others to deceive him; for he rejoices at seemingly possessing goods, whereas, in very deed, he has none at all.

571. Such attachment in a man is more willful than true self-love; it is an inordinate love of the body, at once ill-advised, blind, beastly, and pernicious to himself and to others.

572. Such love Socrates declared to be the head and

beginning of all evils. When mutual love is overthrown, then is born every evil of the human race.

573. He who loves himself excessively according to this pattern loves no man, and is loved by no man in return.

574. The proud man is at variance with the meek, and much more so with the proud.

575. Our Savior in His heavenly wisdom briefly proposes this compendium of what is to be loved and what to be hated, saying generally, "He who seemingly hates his soul, and yet who does not suffer it to be entangled with the pleasant enticements of the world, he truly loves his soul and wills it to be saved. Contrariwise, he who seemingly loves his soul and yet allows it any indulgence, the same hates his soul and wills it to be damned."

576. Who except a madman would refuse labor and pains to obtain the eternal reward in heaven, since decaying and transitory things demand so much labor and pains?

577. The law of Adam's children is to live in labor, and the curse of Eve's offspring is to suffer afflictions and troubles. Therefore, we must labor whatever way we turn.

578. How much better to endeavor with all our power to have for our labor the highest reward, and not that other slender and menial recompense shortly vanishing yet of eternal pain and sorrow!

579. Note, also, that doing good is easier, surer, quieter, and much more pleasant and enjoyable than doing evil, which is full of fear and solicitude.

580. Sin is the death of man: indeed, he may well seem to destroy himself who falls into sin. For he withdraws himself from God, our life; and he turns from that quietness of conscience, than which there is nothing more blessed.

581. Wash away the stains of sin with tears and repentance, and by invocation of the mercy of God, wholely trust in it.

582. Let every occasion of sin be avoided and cut away with all diligence; for the Wise Man says, "He who loves peril shall perish therein."

583. The devil always waits closely for his chance, so that we can never live in security.

584. We must ever do battle with him. "Man's life upon earth is," as Job truly says, "a continual warfare."

585. Our enemy is so mighty, so strong, so subtle, so crafty, has such great experience, and has so many policies of war, such strategies and deceits against us that we can by no means match him. Nor can we surpass him in conflict; therefore, mistrusting our own forces, we ought to flee to God for succor.

586. For this cause Our Lord and Teacher often commands His disciples to pray and to petition the Father of all with devoted wills that they may not be led into temptation—that is to say, into battle or handgrips with their adversary, the devil.

587. In the prayer that He taught us, this is the crown, "Lead us not into temptation," but deliver us from that depraved plotter.

588. Let us, therefore, always do as men armed in war: keep diligent watch and work, not letting occasions

slip away by sleep. Furthermore, since this life flees so fast away, and is of such uncertainty that no man can make sure promise of tomorrow, it is very stupid and foolhardy to put our hopes on a long life—and so not prepare for our final journey. We are called every moment; yet we do not know when we shall be forced to this journey whether we will or no. In view of all we have said, let us prepare a treasure for the life to come, to which something each day might be added. When we shall be called by death, let us not be found unready, or oppressed with heavy and dull sluggishness. Let us not depart sad and sorrowful, but as men prepared and fully satisfied with this world. Let us rejoice in hope beyond ourselves innocently and holily, surpassing ourselves through faith in the Son of God, and with the piety in which by Him we were nourished. Nothing greater or more beautiful can be given to God by man. In Christ we have come to know God. As far as the power of man is able, we imitate, we follow after, and we even sometimes find Him.

589. Without this, what is man but an immortal beast?

590. As one day of man's life is to be preferred to the longest age of raven or hart, so one day lived in religion, that is, one day of divine life, is to be preferred to an eternity without religion.

591. "This is eternal life," says Christ our Lord, "to know the Father and Him Whom He sent, Jesus, His Son."

592. This is the course of absolute wisdom, whose beginning step is to know yourself—and the last of all, to know God.

FINIS

To the immortal and inviolable King of the World, to
God only, be all honor and glory!

MARIAN LEONA TOBRINER, S.N.J.M., received the M.A. in 1960 and the Ph.D. in 1966 from Stanford University. She has held various administrative positions and was Vice Principal and Dean of Ramona Convent High School in Alhambra, California. She is now Visiting Assistant Professor at California State College at Los Angeles, and is currently doing research on the letters between Vives and Erasmus, and on Vives' annotations to the 1522 edition of Augustine's *City of God*.